M000250509

DOWNSIZING

DOWNSIZING

THE 5-STEP METHOD
for Life Transitions Big and Small

MIA DANIELLE

ROCKRIDGE
PRESS

Copyright © 2019 Rockridge Press, Emeryville, California

No part of this publication may be reproduced, stored in a retrieval system, or transmitted in any form or by any means, electronic, mechanical, photocopying, recording, scanning, or otherwise, except as permitted under Sections 107 or 108 of the 1976 United States Copyright Act, without the prior written permission of the Publisher. Requests to the Publisher for permission should be addressed to the Permissions Department, Rockridge Press, 6005 Shellmound Street, Suite 175, Emeryville, CA 94608.

Limit of Liability/Disclaimer of Warranty: The Publisher and the author make no representations or warranties with respect to the accuracy or complete- ness of the contents of this work and specifically disclaim all warranties, including without limitation warranties of fitness for a particular purpose. No warranty may be created or extended by sales or promotional materials. The advice and strategies contained herein may not be suitable for every situation. This work is sold with the understanding that the Publisher is not engaged in rendering medical, legal, or other professional advice or services. If professional assistance is required, the services of a competent professional person should be sought. Neither the Publisher nor the author shall be liable for damages arising herefrom. The fact that an individual, organization, or website is referred to in this work as a citation and/or potential source of further information does not mean that the author or the Publisher endorses the information the individual, organization, or website may provide or recommendations they/it may make. Further, readers should be aware that

websites listed in this work may have changed or disappeared between when this work was written and when it is read.

For general information on our other products and services or to obtain technical support, please contact our Customer Care Department within the United States at (866) 744-2665, or outside the United States at (510) 253-0500.

Rockridge Press publishes its books in a variety of electronic and print formats. Some content that appears in print may not be available in electronic books, and vice versa.

TRADEMARKS: Rockridge Press and the Rockridge Press logo are trademarks or registered trademarks of Callisto Media Inc. and/or its affiliates, in the United States and other countries, and may not be used without written permission. All other trademarks are the property of their respective owners. Rockridge Press is not associated with any product or vendor mentioned in this book.

Interior and Cover Designer: Darren Samuel
Art Producer: Sue Bischofberger
Editor: Rochelle Torke
Production Manager: Riley Hoffman
Production Editor: Melissa Edeburn

ISBN: Print 978-1-64152-862-7 | eBook 978-1-64152-863-4

R0

To my daughters, Abigail and Gracie—
I'm proud to be your mom and share this crazy life with you.

Contents

1 The Downsizing Method

2 Decluttering & Minimalism

The Upside of Downsizing

I was in my mid-twenties with a toddler and a preschooler when my life turned upside down. This wasn't my first life-changing transition and definitely wouldn't be my last. A year after building my dream home I was getting divorced and finally leaving the small Texas town I'd always known. This transition had become an opportunity to hit the open road with my two little girls—no storage to safeguard my belongings because I wouldn't be coming back this time.

After sweating in a dusty storage facility with my sister and her husband (who I had paid with a 60-inch TV that used to hang in my living room), I tossed the last donation item from my old life into the back of the truck. That was it—the final gesture of no return. Downsizing felt like removing armor I had carried around my entire life, leaving me vulnerable, weightless, hopeful.

The idea of reducing clutter is wildly popular now for several reasons, including lowered costs and improved use of space. But it also offers the potential to simplify life. Most of my downsizing clients are busy moms who feel overwhelmed by clutter and want to make better use of their time and energy. For them, the minimalist mind-set—owning fewer possessions—means focusing on the important things in life. They would rather spend time with a person they love than wash loads of dishes and laundry or dust a bunch of knickknacks.

You may be at a pivotal moment that's leading you to downsize—a divorce, a death, a big move. Regardless of your reason, your decision to downsize involves letting go of material possessions.

The process might be difficult or even painful, but it's also liberating because it allows you a fresh start. When you release possessions, you free yourself to look forward. From personal experience, I can tell you that clearing out the clutter creates mental space for new ideas, people, and opportunities.

Making the choice to let go and allow what's next—whether with fear, excitement, or hope—is beautiful. I want to inspire you to see the possibilities and take a chance on realizing them. This book will start you on your path.

How This Book Will Help

This book will guide you through any downsizing situation you may be facing now or in the future. Its 5-step method, with tips and tools, will help you manage moves, divisions of households after breakups or divorce, empty nesting, senior downsizing, tending to estates after a death, and decluttering for a more minimalist lifestyle. You'll likely face one or more of these situations at some point. If you happen to have downsizing circumstances not specifically addressed in this book, know that the methods presented here are still applicable.

In my experience, the practical details of downsizing are rarely the biggest hurdle. It's the attendant emotions that cause many people to stumble. We tend to form attachments to our belongings and hold on to them out of fear. Learning to emotionally release possessions is critical to successfully downsizing.

The following chapters will address the emotions that may arise in a variety of downsizing situations, providing the support you need to make a smooth transition to your downsized life.

1

The Downsizing Method

START WHERE YOU ARE

After years of studying our relationships with our environments—including how we respond to clutter and personal belongings—I can say with certainty that nothing affects our happiness and personal energy as immediately as our surroundings. And what environment affects you more than your personal home space?

Multiple research studies support the correlation between clutter and stress as well as link environments to happiness. That's why I have dedicated a blog and online business to sharing methods to produce clutter-free, energized home spaces.

This journey belongs to you. One mistake I see people make is to compare their starting point with someone else's end. Don't fall into the comparison trap. Remember that everyone who has ever downsized for any reason had to start somewhere.

So what brought you here? Take a moment and really give some thought to the situation that motivated you to read this book today. How do you feel about that situation? Are you downsizing by choice or due to circumstance?

Acknowledging your emotions throughout the process is part of the project of downsizing. Feelings like eagerness, reluctance, and anxiety may affect how quickly you progress through the steps, and how easy or difficult you find them. Pushing feelings aside and charging stoically forward can actually cause you to expend more energy—and might even bring the whole effort to a halt.

Pull out your notebook and start getting your feelings onto paper. In fact, I encourage this practice throughout your downsizing effort. Journaling is therapeutic because it increases self-awareness, which is empowering. Are you feeling sad, energized, or nervous? Self-awareness can prevent your emotions from slowing down your progress.

In later chapters, we'll spend some time addressing emotions that arise in particular life transitions and techniques for processing them so that your downsizing proceeds smoothly.

THE 5-STEP METHOD

The 5-Step Method gives you a structure for downsizing. It was developed to maximize efficiency in a range of situations. Take downsizing after the death of a family member. This situation raises a number of unique issues, such as handling wills and estates, coordinating with other grieving family members, and making decisions within an emotional landscape of loss. All these issues are highly specific, but the 5-Step Method is just as useful in this situation as in other downsizing situations, such as moving houses or dividing households in the wake of a breakup.

The steps are designed to be followed in order. However, as we all know, life sometimes throws us curveballs. It's okay to be flexible. As long as you methodically work through each of the steps, nothing will be left undone.

STEP 1: PLAN SMART

Don't discount the massive importance of this step. Many people make the mistake of diving headfirst into these heavy projects with little to no plan or specific goal in mind—this is a quick way to become overwhelmed or even paralyzed by the process.

Before you dive into sorting and tossing (and find yourself lost in the middle of a pile), you need to take an inventory of the overall project, and define what it is you hope to accomplish.

The Technical Details

Some details of your downsizing affect the project's entire timeline. Use the blank timeline I provide in this chapter's tools (see page 6) to track applicable dates. Additional blank timelines are provided for you in the Tools and Checklists section (pages 123 to 124). Of course, these dates and other details will vary from project to project.

Create Your Vision

Downsizing, like any other task, requires vision and motivation. It's important to understand the "why" that's driving and inspiring your project—and call it to mind on difficult days when the work feels taxing. For example, if you're downsizing to achieve a more minimalist lifestyle, you need to have a good reason for wanting to live clutter-free as well as a clear vision of what your daily life will look and feel like when you accomplish your goal. Even downsizing a loved one's belongings after they've passed away requires a particular vision and purpose. That purpose could be to fulfill the wishes laid out in their will, to sort through your own emotions, or to take some of the burden off other loved ones and help them heal. Your vision could include specific pieces you choose to keep and what you decide to do with them to keep their memory alive for future generations.

Whatever your downsizing situation, take time to fully develop your vision. Record your thoughts in your notebook. Look for inspiration photos and make lists to clarify your vision. You're not etching all future decisions in stone. You're identifying a destination so you can create a map for reaching it.

See the Floor Plan Tool (page 118) to help you think about how you'll arrange your belongings in a new space or how you'd like to rearrange a part of your home. This grid will help you create a scaled floor plan for the room or rooms you wish to transform.

It works best if you measure your furniture and your space first and try to keep yourself honest about the dimensions. Many of us have probably convinced ourselves that we could squeeze more furniture into a space than would actually fit. A tape measure is a true ally, preventing the kind of wishful thinking that could turn into big headaches later.

Identify Your Timeline

Some situations require a tight and highly specific due date, such as moving to a new home or going through wills and estates after a death in the family. Other situations may be more open-ended, like decluttering your home for a more minimalist lifestyle, or downsizing your college-age child's belongings after they've flown the coop.

If there's a hard deadline, mark it on your timeline or calendar. Projects with an actual due date have a higher rate of success. When everything is open-ended, procrastination sets in, and it's easier to quit when things seem difficult. Make this project real by assigning a deadline, even if outside forces don't demand it. As C. N. Parkinson said: "Work expands so as to fill the time available for its completion," or, in other words, the more time you give yourself, the longer it will take.

Take an Inventory

You don't need to physically count how many items you're about to sort. However, take an observational inventory for a sense of how big the project is actually going to be. Take into account how many rooms you'll be going through and how much stuff (percentage or otherwise) will need downsizing. Decide if you require any temporary storage space or transportation needs like a truck rental.

For example, knowing you need to downsize by around 50 percent prepares you to be more ruthless in making discards.

PLANNING CHECKLIST

○ Articulate the goals and the vision behind your downsizing project.

○ Set a start and end date for your work, including a date for each major task involved.

○ Determine the size of the project:_____(number of rooms or percentage to be downsized).

○ Develop your vision for the future space using the blank floor plan and your book/journal.

BLANK TIMELINE

Here's a blank one-month timeline you can use to set a schedule for any downsizing project. Simply enter your start date and end date and record your action steps for each week of the month. You'll find additional copies of this tool on pages 123 to 124.

Example Timeline

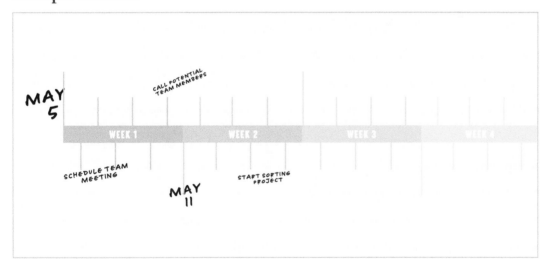

Project 1

START DATE   **END DATE**

Project 2

START DATE   **END DATE**

Project 3

START DATE   **END DATE**

You may think it seems silly to recruit a team for just decluttering your home, but a "team" can be as small as you and a friend or your spouse and kids. Aside from the obvious labor-intensive assistance you might need, the accountability that comes with involving just one other person can be powerful.

Also, even if you're a type-A personality who prefers to maintain control in all situations, recruiting a team to share some of the load can be a huge relief and will save hours of your time. Whether moving to a new home or decluttering, the process is more enjoyable when you're working with a team.

Write a list of people you would like to include in each step of the process. Mentally work through the phases of the project (sorting, boxing, hauling, etc.) and identify who would be a good fit for each one. For the sorting phase, for example, select a trusted friend to help you make big decisions about what to keep and what to ditch. Sometimes we need a good friend to tell us that the 70s called and want our lamps back. For the hauling phase, select friends who can do donation drop-offs and any other activities requiring heavy lifting.

This brainstorming exercise will give you more clarity and composure when you decide to reach out to them. Use your notebook and pen or one of the tools in this chapter to help plan your ideal team.

Share Your Vision with Care

Keep in mind that all the items at stake may not necessarily be yours. They may also belong to your spouse, your kids, roommates, or other family members who happen to share the space. It's important to have a shared vision of the end result, so be sure to acknowledge others' feelings, opinions, and ideas. Communicate clearly with everyone involved, so each person has the same understanding of expectations and goals and can agree on decisions.

This is especially true with children who might be participating in sorting and downsizing their own belongings but still need a bit more guidance. Explain the expectations in straightforward language and offer bite-size instructions. Simple tasks are best; for example, you might have them put a white sticker on the things they want to keep, and then place specific items in boxes.

If you're moving homes, share your vision and expectations for the new home. How? If you're downsizing your child's room into a guest room after the child moves out, for instance, share the vision for this open space with your spouse or partner, or another child still living at home, whatever the case may be. (Maybe they've always wanted to sit in that window and daydream!)

If helping a senior parent downsize to a more accommodating living situation, be sure to point out the positives of the transition and how it will help enhance their daily life. When you take the time to communicate and share the vision with all involved participants, the entire process will move along more smoothly, and may even bring you closer together.

One situation that can be tricky is working through wills and estates with other family members with whom you may not regularly communicate. While we'll go into more detail on the specifics of this situation in chapter 6, keep in mind that it's important to maintain an open line of communication and schedule a time for each person concerned to participate.

Team Coordination

Before you invite helpers, consider how you can turn the project into a fun event. I've found that people are highly motivated by food—turning a request for assistance into a pizza party or offering free snacks can make the idea of providing hard labor more palatable.

Consider creative ways to involve friends or members of your community. For example, you might host a swap party, and invite friends to bring items of interest (clothing or Tupperware are common) to exchange with others. You might simply offer that whoever helps is free to take whatever item they like from the donation pile.

Use the following tools to assemble your team, assign tasks, and schedule task dates.

TEAM BUILDING STEPS

Step 1: Determine your team needs.

- Think about each project phase and which helper might be suited to it. Once you've identified teammates, assign them to tasks using the lines below.

- Brainstorm names of potential teammates and assign them to tasks using the list below.

- Decide if there will be a special event to entice people to show up (pizza party, etc.).

- Decide on a date or a few available dates for this to take place.

Team 1: Sorting

_____

_____

_____

_____

_____

Team 2: Moving and Hauling

_____

_____

_____

_____

_____

Team 3: Other: _____

_____

_____

_____

_____

Step 2: Invite your helpers.

- Call each person on the lists above and insert the names of those able to help in the Team Assignments Tool on page 10.

Step 3: Complete the Team Assignments Tool.

- In the Preparation column, write down any special activities, food, or other perks for your team. Use the other columns to note the date and time of tasks and the names of task helpers.

TEAM ASSIGNMENTS TOOL

DATE AND TIME	EVENT OR TASK	HELPER	PREPARATIONS

STEP 3: THE BIG SORT

The great thing about formulating a detailed vision is that it makes the sorting process much easier. Once you've gained clarity in envisioning your end goal, it's time to get physical and go through your belongings. You may want to dive in and spread everything out across the floor—but wait! There's a system for sorting.

I've already mentioned some common mistakes, and here is another big one: unloading all your belongings and attempting to plunge into the entire project all at once. This is because walking into a room full of clutter immediately overwhelms your mind and leads to confusion. It's no surprise that people often become totally frozen in place by the process at this point. In short, don't empty any bins or boxes just yet.

SORTING TOOLS

- Any packing equipment necessary
- Boxes or bags to tote
- Garbage bags
- Notebook
- Pen/pencil
- Sticker dots
- Tape (if using boxes)

Items to Keep

The first step to sorting for any downsizing situation is to choose which items to keep. Don't try to sort out your donation items at the same time. Approach this task as though you have on blinders that allow you to see only the items you already know you want.

Be Selective

"Selecting" is an act of intention, so begin by choosing only those items you wish to keep; in particular, focus on ones that fit in with the vision you've created for your future environment.

This is exactly how we packed for our most recent big move. We kept our eye on the ball (i.e., the stuff we were keeping). I didn't worry about the mess left behind because everything that remained would be discarded. The process of going back and scooping up the discards was incredibly simple, because we'd already made the tough decisions regarding what to keep.

So, at this moment in the process, don't worry about what will be donated or sold. One simple method that works for any situation is to sort your belongings with stickers. To use this method, get a packet of multicolored sticker dots. Put a white sticker on the items to be kept—white is simple and generally easy to spot. The other colors you'll use later.

When you begin by focusing on items to keep, you'll find it's much easier to let go of possessions you aren't keeping. On the other hand, when you begin by sorting everything simultaneously, you naturally end up tossing more items into the "keep pile" than needed. You might want to make a list of the selected items to keep using a notebook or spreadsheet. This is especially helpful when moving and labeling boxes or accounting for items claimed from an estate or will.

Alternative Ways to Save Keepsakes

There's more than one way to keep an item. If you're finding that your "keep pile" is larger than you'd like it to be, consider other options. For example, don't discount the value of photos and videos for preserving memories (see page 14 for additional suggestions).

Recently Facebook kindly sent a reminder of some childhood photos of my little sister and me. We were sporting red cowgirl hats and tan faux-leather pants with fringe spilling down the sides. These photos made two truths loud and clear: As a kid, I was not nearly as cute as I thought I was, and I don't need to hold on to my own kid's adorable clothes to get a kick out of the memory.

Of course, there are more options than snapping a picture. A while back I was asked to speak at a virtual event for widows about decluttering after a death. Going through the belongings of a lost spouse is uniquely painful, but I walked away from that event inspired by some of the things these women had done to preserve precious items. One woman had taken pieces of her husband's favorite clothes and patched them together to create a teddy bear. There are so many ways you can use multiple pieces or parts to create a new whole; many of these can be used for décor or other practical daily integration like a quilt.

Items to Let Go

Now that all your "keep" items are labeled and set aside—congratulations, the hardest part is over! Everything left is going somewhere else, so it's just a matter of deciding where. The remainder of the sticker dots should be marked as one of these three categories: donate, sell, or toss.

Don't make this particular step any harder than it needs to be—this can be as simple as walking around and placing stickers on things. (We'll tend to the manual work of moving things around and processing the sales later.) However, you should keep separate lists or spreadsheets of the items to be donated and sold—you'll find the tools to do just that in this chapter (see pages 16 and 20).

Donate It

If you're worried about being wasteful by giving away perfectly good items, I want to encourage you to reframe your mind-set. Giving is never a waste. Consider the item you haven't been using, which is taking up good square footage in your home (space you've paid good money for). This item is no longer fulfilling a purpose. The material used to create it, the hours put into its conception, and its general essence are all being wasted as it sits unused. Which is more wasteful: continuing to store it, or giving it to someone who can actually use it?

You might give items to a family member or friend who would use them; donate them to a group cause such as a community yard sale, a community collection at a library, or a museum; or, most commonly, to a dedicated donation center.

The latter tends to be easiest because all items are boxed or bagged and delivered to a single location. Donation centers across the world support various causes, so you have the option to select one that's personally meaningful to you. In addition, most large donation centers now offer free pickups, which makes this option even more enticing.

Sell It

We'll go into more detail on the methods of selling items of value in a different step. For now, just identify these items by placing a colored sticker on them and keep a written list or ledger of the items to sell as you mark them—you'll use this later to keep track of sales.

Toss It

I know that nobody wants to be wasteful, but there are some items you cannot donate or sell and therefore must be tossed. It's actually less wasteful to toss something that can't be used by others (and isn't being used by you) than it is to waste your space, time, and energy.

We tend to attribute more value to items we own just because we own them. There's a name for this thinking: the Endowment Effect. This is a psychological hiccup that causes us to unreasonably overvalue something that belongs to us despite its true market value. Be conscious of this effect and don't allow it to hinder your progress.

PRESERVING MEMORIES: OTHER OPTIONS

The following provide excellent alternatives for holding on to memories without taking up valuable space. They also make meaningful gifts for the family.

- Artwork binder
- Digital photos
- Mural
- Quilt from cloth
- Patched stuffed animal from cloth
- Picture frame or décor (from jewelry)
- Scrapbook
- Screen saver/digital picture frame
- Videos

STEP 4: DONATE, SELL, OR TOSS

Once you've assembled your team and sorted your items, it's finally time to get those items out the door. This is where your hard work pays off. You'll start to feel relief as you see things go to their respective locations, and space begins to open up.

After all your diligent work, you can now begin to feel good about the donations and gifts you're giving and the new stream of income from the items you're selling. All the tough decisions have already been made—this is the easy part.

Because your items are now organized and marked, you only need to refer to the colored sticker system and start routing things to their ultimate destinations. Be sure to add any donation pickup dates, selling meetings, or trash pickups to your timeline as you plan (see page 6).

Donating

When we first started downsizing our belongings—for the sake of owning less junk—I decided to go a different route from our usual Goodwill trips. We had accumulated about 50 bags of random family goods—blankets, toys, furniture, etc. A quick Google search showed me a list of the many donation centers in my area, some of which were willing to come and pick up a haul this size (see list of donation sites below).

I chose the Vietnam Veterans of America (VVA) because I liked the idea of helping those families. They accept all types of diverse items, and their scheduling process is incredibly easy (simply go to their website and sign up for an available date and time). All I had to do was leave the bags outside the front door on the scheduled date. This meant no bugging a relative with a truck or making multiple trips to a drop-off site in my SUV.

When it comes to giving or donating, you can make the experience as personal as you like. There are numerous qualified charities and donating options (for specifics consider seeking the advice of a tax specialist or check out the latest rules surrounding donations in the United States at www.irs.gov). Some specialize in specific types of items, such as clothing and baby supplies for women and children's shelters, suits and dresswear for formerly incarcerated people interviewing for jobs, toiletries for homeless LGBTQ+ youth, books for the library, or toys for group homes, but another consideration is your own convenience. Sometimes our timelines demand that we get things done quickly and efficiently. In the end, consider all the factors that make a particular option best for your situation.

DONATION SITES

- Community (libraries, houses of worship, schools)
- Foster homes/group homes
- Goodwill
- Habitat for Humanity
- Local charities
- Savers
- Homeless shelters
- Senior centers
- VVA (Vietnam Veterans of America)
- Women's shelters

TAX-DEDUCTIBLE DONATIONS TRACKER

ITEM TYPE	QUANTITY	DONATION CENTER	DATE	ESTIMATED VALUE OF EACH	TOTAL ESTIMATED VALUE

Selling

If you haven't yet tapped into the wonderful world of selling your stuff online, you're missing out on some easy cash. Tons of apps with new options are popping up each day. Depending on where you live, some will have a higher presence in your area. Do a bit of research to see which apps/sites have the largest population of use in your location—this will mean more eyes on the items you're trying to sell.

Of course, you still have in-person options like garage sales, yard sales, and consignment shops. However, for the amount of effort and return, selling via websites and apps gives you more money for your time, and requires far less labor than waking up at 4:00 a.m. to sit in a hot garage for hours so that strangers can nickel-and-dime you.

Top-Selling Apps and Sites

I've provided a list of popular online retailers (see page 18), but to get you started, I want to share a few of my personal favorites and how they work. My top three preferred apps are OfferUp, letgo, and Craigslist. Good old eBay is still alive and kicking, but it hasn't been a top player in the "selling your stuff world" for a while. However, if you have antiques or unopened boxes of value, or old electronics, eBay is great for selling or pricing niche items of that kind. For example, if someone is collecting original G. I. Joe action figures—still in the box, unopened, like the ones you just found in your attic— eBay would be the place to check pricing.

Craigslist is big. There are probably more people on Craigslist right now than any of the apps you can download on your phone. However, with thousands of people using the site, and very little security built into the platform, you have to be careful.

On OfferUp you can snap a photo right from your phone, then add a title, a quick description, and a price. The process only takes seconds, and the photo is added to the feed for people to see. You can also choose to make it available by mail, so your item reaches a wider audience. The site verifies each person—even going so far as to check driver's licenses—and has a good review system. As long as the person on the other end has a green check of verification and positive reviews, you can rest easy.

Letgo is almost identical to OfferUp. This is one of those cases where it just depends on which site has a higher presence in your location. Again, do your research and find the option that works best for you.

Many people have turned to Facebook Marketplace or local Facebook buying/selling groups, and they become more popular every day. While there are no buyer protections here, either, at the very least, your wheeling and dealing is being done in a semi-public forum, rather than relatively anonymously, like on Craigslist.

Getting the Most from Your Post

Regardless of which app or website you end up using, here are a few tips to help you get the most bang for your buck:

1. Make sure you have good lighting—natural lighting is best.

2. Take vertical pictures instead of landscape—photos in this format take up more space in the feed, which makes them more visible.

3. Start high with your price, and lower it each day or so until you find a buyer.

Throughout the four steps leading up to this point, I've identified different tasks to track. Now Step 5 is all about gathering that data to track your progress as well as the items you're letting go.

ONLINE RETAILERS

- Amazon Seller Central
- Craigslist
- Decluttr
- eBay
- Etsy
- Facebook Marketplace
- letgo
- Nextdoor
- OfferUp

STEP 5: KEEP TRACK

As a kid, I helped my mother haul garbage bags full of clothes, swing sets, and toys into the garage. I taped handmade price tags onto tables and sat patiently, waiting for customers to arrive. My job was to be the cashier and inventory tracker. No fifty-cent purchase made its way out of our garage without a check mark from me.

At the time I didn't understand why it was necessary to keep track of things—I mean, *why not just take the money and go*? It reminded me an awful lot of helping my dad track inventory in the parts department of his car dealership. We even used the same giant yellow legal pads.

It turns out the reasons are actually similar. All businesses are required to report sales and income; you should do the same for items sold out of your own home. On your annual taxes, it may benefit you to claim certain items.

In Step 5 of your downsizing project, you'll use the data you gathered in steps 1 through 4 to track your progress and the items you're letting go.

Recording What Went Where

Here you'll find a few tools to help you track the possessions you've donated, sold, or discarded.

Tracking Your Donations and Sales

As already mentioned, tracking donations and sales may benefit you on your annual income taxes, and in some cases, this may even be required. You may be able to count certain donations as deductibles, which will require you to provide a breakdown of the individual items donated and their estimated value. Companies like Goodwill will give you a receipt to include with your taxes but won't include an itemized breakdown—you'll need to do that on your own.

In some situations, sold items must be claimed on tax reports, as well. In any case, it's nice to see how much income you're raking in. This information can help you make decisions about future purchases and sales. Resale value is part of the overall value of an item, and you get to see firsthand which belongings have a solid resale value. Also, if you're selling items for family members (spouse, kids, etc.), keeping a ledger will make it easier to divvy out payments.

One of the tools included in this chapter is a ledger for tracking sales (see page 20).

SALES LEDGER

ITEM	LIST PRICE	SOLD VIA	DATE	SELL PRICE

READY, SET, GO!

Now that you understand the 5-Step Method, you're ready to connect it to your particular downsizing situation. And as we mentioned, the rest of the chapters in this book offer details specific to common downsizing scenarios: decluttering and embracing minimalism, moving, dividing a household after a breakup or divorce, cleaning out empty nests, senior downsizing, and downsizing after a death (taking care of wills and estates).

If you've been particularly struck by certain ideas or had lightbulbs go off while reading through these steps, go ahead and write them down in your notebook so they don't get lost.

While you can jump to the chapter that relates to your current downsizing situation, I recommend that you study the opening sections of each chapter, which are each entitled "The Task Ahead" and summarize what's to come. All the chapters contain information that is relevant to a variety of circumstances. So, while you may be currently focusing on a specific downsizing scenario discussed in one chapter, you may still find other parts of the book helpful.

2

Decluttering & Minimalism

THE TASK AHEAD

Interest in minimalism—and the mass exodus of clutter from households in many parts of the world—is on the rise. Many of us now understand that a cluttered environment feels overwhelming. It also means we're wasting our rent or mortgage to house items that give us little in return.

Still, I've worked with enough people to know that even those who truly want to declutter and simplify their home spaces often find it challenging. They don't know where to start or how to let go of their possessions. This chapter will break down that process and motivate you to stick with the big task of going small.

THE LOGISTICS OF DECLUTTERING

Keep it simple. Too often people will overcomplicate the process of decluttering their belongings because it's easier to create a complex organization system than to actually let things go. If you truly want to declutter and minimize your belongings, adopt the motto, "I don't need more storage, I need less stuff!"

We'll discuss the emotions behind the process shortly but, for now, follow the five steps detailed in chapter 1 to keep the process simple. It might be tempting to *just dive in* and skip the planning phase altogether, but the excitement of getting started won't last as long as the project itself. What *will* endure—and propel you forward when things get difficult—is your vision for your space and your "why."

For example, decluttering your dining room because you're tired of seeing your dining table used as a catch-all is enough to get you chucking things into a donation box. At first, you just want the stuff gone. However, as soon as you begin to get tired, that initial motivation will likely die down, and things will go back to the way they were.

On the other hand, if you decide to declutter your dining room because you feel you don't see your kid(s) or partner enough, and you want to start having dinner together every night at the table, that is a far more powerful goal. Goals like this—goals with intention and vision—will keep you motivated. Similarly, envisioning yourself sipping your morning coffee at a spacious, clutter-free, cozy kitchen nook while the rest of the world is still asleep is a powerful vision. The more heartfelt the reason, and the more detailed the vision, the more successful you'll have in achieving it.

Create a Timeline

When decluttering for your own personal reasons without a hard deadline, the job can drag on indefinitely. This is one of those situations where you must be your own manager and create your own timeline (see the blank timeline tool on page 6). Remember, if it isn't on the schedule, it isn't real.

Start by checking your calendar for some available space you can dedicate to your decluttering project. It's important that you set yourself up for success from the very beginning. Planning this process during a period when you are already committed to numerous other activities will only waste your time and discourage you.

Self-awareness is huge during this part of the process. We all have times of the day, week, and month when we have highs or lows in our energy. If you try planning your decluttering sessions at 5:00 a.m., when you know you're a night owl who's never up before 9:00 a.m., your timeline might as well be a work of fiction.

Also, determine if you'll be needing help and, if so, from whom? (see Step 2: Build Your Team, page 7). Do your best to determine the availability of those people before creating a hard timeline or breaking down the schedule for your project.

Once all the factors have been cleared and confirmed, enter the start date and due date on your timeline. All of the details and tedious dates that come up during the planning process can be filled in as you go. You now have parameters for setting up those other details, which can only be scheduled between your fixed start and end.

Gather Your Tools

For decluttering and minimizing your belongings, you'll want to use the following aids in the Tools and Checklists section (page 117):

- Floor plan tool
- Planning checklist
- Moving checklist
- Blank timeline
- Writing prompt for selecting items to keep
- Team Building Steps

- Team Assignments Tool
- Donation sites
- Tax-deductible donations tracker
- List of online retailers
- Belongings tracker
- Sales ledger
- Overall project timeline

Take the First Step

I get asked quite a lot about where and how to start decluttering. I recommend beginning with the bedroom. This is the space most personally connected to you, the most authentic and private space most of us possess. Your bedroom is the last place you see before you close your eyes at night and the first place you set eyes on in the morning.

Your bedroom affects your energy and mood for the rest of the day. When you close your eyes feeling safe and peaceful, you rest better and your brain recharges more efficiently. The next morning, when you open your eyes to a space that inspires you, this lifts your mood and you feel invigorated.

Because you've started your day on the right foot, you'll have more energy and momentum to face the day. This not only helps the clutter-free lifestyle take root, but it encourages you to extend this peaceful state into other areas of your home.

Too often, bedrooms are treated as an afterthought: where excess boxes and belongings are thrown to be kept "out of sight," piles of laundry are heaped, and candy wrappers are discarded next to contents of emptied pockets on bedside tables. But the way you treat your most personal space says something about how you value yourself. The belongings you keep indicate what you're willing to tolerate in your life.

Right now, the first step might be defining your plan and gathering your materials. Decide what packing materials or resources you need to get started—boxes, garbage bags, etc.—and focus on getting those ready. However, the moment will arrive when there's nothing left to do but begin.

THE EMOTIONS OF DECLUTTERING

Acknowledging your emotions regarding your possessions will help you move forward. Avoiding unpleasant emotions, on the other hand, only leads to rationalization and self-sabotage. This is why so many people accept defeat when they truly do want to declutter and simplify.

Our minds are programmed to keep us safe, which means steering clear of uncertainty. If you avoid the true emotional reason for your clutter, you could find justifications for keeping all your belongings.

So ask yourself: Why do I have clutter? There are typically three emotional reasons we tend to collect and hold on to belongings: fear, sentiment, and apathy and avoidance.

1. Fear

The most common reason is fear—of the future and also of losing touch with the past. Fear of the future is captured in the adage, "Better to have it and not need it than to need it and not have it." That misguided logic allows you to collect items—who's to say you won't need them someday!—and, as often as not, quickly forget you have them.

Fear of losing touch with the past is often confused with sentiment, but these items aren't truly sentimental. These are random pieces collected out of the fear that a particular memory will be forgotten, or a piece of old identity will be lost. An example might be holding on to an old cheerleader uniform from decades ago, or storing all of your children's old clothes in bins in the garage.

2. Sentimentality

Sentimental items, on the other hand, are items of true and specific emotional value. These are often things like old love letters, your mother's necklace, a 30-day chip from AA, family heirlooms, and the like. Because sentiment is completely subjective, self-awareness and honesty are key. There's nothing wrong with keeping a sentimental item that holds meaning to you, no more than there is eating one candy bar. But what about 50 candy bars?

3. Apathy and Avoidance

It's stressful to focus on the problem, so instead, you go numb and ignore it. Apathy is just a form of avoidance and many other emotions can be hiding behind it, such as anxiety, guilt, or simply feeling overwhelmed. A habit of falling out of action can also manifest in less insidious ways, sometimes masquerading as politeness: someone gives you a gift you don't particularly like but you keep it anyway—because you don't want to hurt their feelings.

Obligation and guilt regarding gifts received, family heirlooms, or items you spent a lot of money on can lead to unnecessary waste of space and emotion. A gift has served its purpose the moment you receive it. And if an item you spent a lot of money on isn't serving its purpose, recognize and acknowledge that it was important once, then sell it or pass it on to someone in need.

I used to hate getting greeting cards because I never knew what to do with them! Some were beautiful and so thoughtful, but I didn't want to devote an entire drawer in my home to every Easter, Birthday, Christmas, Halloween, and Thank You. These things pile up quickly. Eventually, I made peace with the fact that the intention and love the card-giver intended was fulfilled the moment I read it, and from then on I discarded greeting cards quickly afterward. It's true that for many people, handwritten notes are very hard to throw away—especially if they're from a relative or friend departed—but you have to set real boundaries around things like these.

The most common weakness that hinders progress in decluttering is the failure to set boundaries. Your belongings should all have boundaries (a specific home for each category), but your boundaries with people are just as important. Weak boundaries can present themselves as uncontrolled impulse buys, or allowing your grown children to use your home as a storage facility. Boundaries are the lifeblood of a clutter-free and streamlined home.

Gains and Losses

You can't choose one thing without rejecting something else. If you choose to go to college to become a doctor, you're rejecting the option of studying engineering. For every "yes," there is always a potential "no."

You can allow these rejections to occur passively or take the reins and make intentional decisions about them. Minimalists choose to reject unnecessary belongings and devote their time, energy, and money elsewhere.

If you counted all the dollars spent per year on material purchases, minutes spent tending to those items (cleaning, repairing, changing batteries, sorting, and organizing), and all the energy devoted to those tasks, how much would it all amount to?

You can see how living a clutter-free or minimalistic life can benefit your finances and freedom, but there are further-reaching benefits you may not have even considered. For example, it's better for the environment. Less clutter means less consumption, which means less material dumped into our landfills.

Also, research has shown that clutter-free living actually has a pretty profound impact on your health! It decreases your daily stress levels, while keeping home spaces free from hidden bacteria, mold, and allergens that affect breathing and cause illness.

Whatever reasons brought you here, keep them front and center as you go through your belongings and make your discards. One thing we know for sure: There are more gains than losses.

Preserving Your Memories

As mentioned in Step 3: The Big Sort (see page 11), there are other ways to preserve your memories than keeping whole items. Sentimental articles of clothing or other fabric items can be broken into pieces and used to create a single functional piece like a quilt; trinkets, charms, and little knickknacks can be made into décor items such as picture frames. And rather than building clutter by holding on to physical objects, keep memories alive via photos or videos of those objects.

The most common type of clutter when downsizing to a more minimalist lifestyle tends to be paper. Some papers are informational, like manuals, statements, bills, policies, and general junk mail. In most cases, digitizing such papers and utilizing online options, like paperless billing, is best, and recycle everything you can. (For old bank or credit card statements, and anything with your account numbers on it, however, shred these items to prevent identity theft.)

However, some papers also hold sentimental value, like school accolades, kids' artwork, projects from your own childhood, photos, cards, letters, etc. For these types of papers, you might preserve the physical copies using a scrapbook, a binder with plastic sleeves, or implementing a memory box. A clutter-free option would be to digitize these and display them as your screensaver, in a digital picture frame, or to create an online album or book. If you go the physical route, be sure to use archival products meant *specifically* for preservation, which will be marked as such and made of acid-free paper. And if you're digitizing, make sure you back those files up on physical hard drives (preferably two, with one stored in a different location), and/or to a cloud-based service, like iCloud or Google Drive.

YOUR NEXT STEPS

I encourage you to push through any uncomfortable emotions that may persist during the process of letting go. Be intentional about what you reject and what you include in your vision for the future—the power to choose is in your hands. Remember that this is your space and it will impact your energy and happiness on a daily basis.

At this point, you should have an established timeline with clear beginning and end dates for your project. Refer back to this timeline throughout the process to keep things moving forward; add new dates as needed. Also, dig deep into your personal reasons for embarking on this project and take the time to follow along with the tools and prompts from Step 1: Plan Smart (see page 3).

Detailing your plan, identifying your vision, and working through your emotions rather than working around them will help you develop a strong foundation to prevent any future rebound. In reading this chapter, you've likely identified some logistical and emotional obstacles that have kept you stuck in the past. Now you have the tools and knowledge to take your next steps forward.

Go back to chapter 1 and work your way through the 5-Step Method. If at any time you feel overwhelmed, take a short break, go for a walk, or grab a meal. It's okay! This chapter probably brought to light a lot of new ideas you haven't considered before, thoughts on your emotional links to your clutter and new methods of downsizing. Let this knowledge fortify you as you embrace a new way of living—think of having more time, freedom, peace, and daily energy.

FEELINGS CHECKLIST

I have a friend who used to be terrified of roller coasters. As a kid, he would stand next to the rides and promptly decline any invitations to join—*Nope, this ride doesn't look like fun anyway; I'm fine right here on the ground*—then watch as his friends laughed and flung their hands in the air at 120 mph.

He continued this for the majority of the day—walking in the hot sun from one attraction to the next, standing in exhaustively long lines, and watching the main attraction from the sidelines. Finally, he began thinking about the reality of the situation: Hundreds of kids had ridden these roller coasters and gotten off totally unharmed. The idea of trying it himself felt uncomfortable and unnerving, but examining the scenario as a purely logical probability allowed him to reconsider it. The next ride nobody invited him to join, but he walked up to the line to board the ride and took the plunge. That day he rode his first roller coaster, and he hasn't been afraid of them since.

As in my friend's case of pushing through his fears, your mind-set is everything when it comes to following through and pushing past emotions that may surface during this process. Your brain is changing the way it's used to viewing your belongings and the way you're accustomed to interacting with your home environment.

Sometimes you'll feel excited and motivated, while other times you'll feel uncertain and fearful of letting something go or making a mistake. Your brain may try to turn to worst-case scenarios. This is all part of the process. With each possession you release and each emotion you work through, the process will get easier and feel safer. The only way to arrive at your ultimate goal is to go through this.

Here are some of the emotions you might experience:

- Confusion
- Exuberance
- Fear
- Fondness
- Guilt
- Hope
- Humor

- Inspiration
- Irritation
- Relief
- Sadness
- Uncertainty
- Worry

Identify any of the emotions you undergo throughout this process and understand that these feelings are normal—not something to avoid. If additional emotions that aren't listed here surface, write them down in your journal, then face them head-on and just allow them to *be*.

WHAT'S ON YOUR MIND?

Use this space to take notes, vent your feelings, or take stock of your
current situation.

_____

_____

_____

_____

_____

_____

_____

_____

_____

_____

_____

_____

_____

_____

_____

_____

_____

_____

_____

_____

_____

3

Moving to a New Home

THE TASK AHEAD

I would go so far as to say that moving is a passion of mine, although I understand why most people don't share my enthusiasm. Since I was seventeen, the longest I've lived in one residence is about three years. Throughout my adult life, I've experienced a wide range of moving situations: relocating to new states where I knew no one, moving back and forth to previous locations with family or friends, upsizing, downsizing, and everything in between. I've moved alone, with just the kids, and as a family.

I've also experienced living in various types of dwellings: apartments, rented rooms, houses I've built and bought, and now a recently purchased condo.

Each move—even those following unpleasant circumstances—was exciting and full of potential, because I feel that moving is an opportunity for a new beginning. Whether you're downsizing your home or just your belongings, this is a chance for a fresh start.

Keep in mind that what you surround yourself with on a daily basis becomes a part of you. I've always thought of our homes as storybooks, sharing little pieces of who we are. Moving houses is a great time to update your story: out with the old and in with bright, new possibilities.

Before you jump into sorting and boxing, think about the reason for your upcoming move. What are the circumstances at play and your emotions attached to these circumstances? Consider your motivation for downsizing for this move. Are you moving to a smaller space? How far are you traveling? Will you need to rent equipment or hire professionals? Having a solid awareness of the details will give clarity to the project and make the planning process straightforward and simple.

This chapter will break down the logistics of downsizing your belongings while moving houses. It will guide you through simple steps to keep the process surging forward and offer tools to ensure that you get the most out of this transition to a new home.

THE LOGISTICS OF MOVING

When moving, it's even more important that you maintain your focus on the "keep pile" as discussed in Step 3: The Big Sort (see page 11). This simplifies the process as the remaining unboxed items will be easily scooped up and discarded. Simply walk through your home labeling the chosen pieces with a white sticker and begin filling boxes.

At this point, you can totally disregard any items you're leaving behind (aside from moving them out of the boxing zone). The only variance is that in Step 3: The Big Sort we were selecting items to stay, and this time you're choosing items to *go* (with you). This is an important distinction, because the belongings you select will need to be packed, transported, and "rehomed" in your new location.

This time, more planning should go into your selection process as you need to be thinking on two different levels and asking two distinct questions: Which items can logistically be moved and physically fit into the new location? Which items fit into your overall vision? The latter is conceptual and is at the heart of your planning in Step 1: Plan Smart (see page 3).

Remember, this is an amazing (and often rare) opportunity to recreate your home space and lifestyle. Plan what type of energy you'll want to feel in each room of your new home: energized, relaxed, inspired—it's your choice. Take the time to truly think about what your future goals and routines will be in your new home and how you can create spaces that support the flow of those activities.

Perhaps you want a workspace that inspires you, a bathroom with a relaxed spa vibe, and a cosmopolitan chic feel in the living area. The pieces that you choose to bring along with you should coordinate with your future vision. If you don't consider these things now (and instead, choose to put it off), you'll likely never see this vision come to life.

Depending on the number of boxes and your spatial limitations, you might need to stack them against the wall in their respective rooms. For our recent move, we were able to stack the boxes right next to the entryway. Because we don't have a huge number of material possessions, this worked out just fine.

Also, you'll likely have items still in use that aren't ready to be boxed. As long as these are clearly marked with a white sticker, there's no need to worry that they'll accidentally be discarded. Once the goods are boxed and placed to the side, you can begin marking your discards to donate, sell, or toss. This method of pulling the "keep" items first and then sorting and discarding what's left simplifies the entire process.

Create a Timeline

Moving houses requires additional preparation compared to other downsizing situations. Of course, the degree of preparation involved depends on the details of the move. For example, moving down the street calls for different considerations than moving across the country.

In any case, you'll almost always have a hard deadline and a specific timeline, so schedule necessary appointments and get them on the timeline as soon as possible. You will find a blank timeline for this purpose in the Tools and Checklists section (pages 123 to 124). Transferring service for utilities like electric, gas, cable, and Internet—and potentially scheduling technician visits—might need more time than expected. The sooner you can get these scheduled, the smoother your transition will be.

You may also find yourself needing to open and close accounts or change subscriptions—bank, gym, local community centers—as well as to register kids to new schools, or settle into a new job. All the daily details of our lives emerge during the moving process, so leave plenty of space for unexpected issues to surface. Remember that your timeline is your friend; it will allow you to view upcoming events at a glance.

You'll also need to schedule any moving-specific services: renting moving trucks, recruiting movers or helpers, and gathering equipment like a dolly and boxes. Because there are so many categories of events that need scheduling, I recommend you go through each of them by group. To help you along, you'll see a moving checklist divided by category in the Tools and Checklists section (page 122). Follow this checklist as you work through Step 1: Plan Smart (see page 3). Again, be sure to add all these dates onto your calendar and timeline as you go.

Gather Your Tools

When moving to a new home, use these tools, found in the Tools and Checklists section (pages 117 to 135), to stay on track:

- Floor plan tool
- Planning checklist
- Moving checklist
- Blank timeline
- Writing prompt for selecting

  items to keep
- Team building steps
- Team assignments tool

- Donation sites
- Tax-deductible donations tracker
- List of online retailers
- Belongings tracker
- Sales ledger
- Overall project timeline: track

  your progress

For moving, in particular, you'll likely use all these tools. The moving checklist will help you transfer services and manage the many other details of a location change. Use it in coordination with the planning checklist for the best results.

Take the First Step

Begin with your timeline tool (see page 6) and moving checklist. Getting things scheduled and squared away will free your mind to really focus on your vision and ideas for your new digs. So, make the necessary phone calls, mark everything on the timeline to cement the plan, and then allow yourself to rest and switch into creative mode.

Draft your vision (using the blank floor plan on page 118 and your notebook) before sorting and boxing. The clarity that will come from having a well-defined end goal will make the sorting process go more smoothly.

THE EMOTIONS OF MOVING

The emotions associated with moving homes are as diverse as the potential moving scenarios. Maybe you just bought a new house and are proudly stepping out into the world of home ownership; or perhaps you're finally taking the plunge and moving to an exciting new location you've always dreamed about. Moving can be exciting, empowering, and hopeful, but that's not always the case. Sometimes the circumstances are unpleasant, like when moving after the loss of a job, the failure of a business, or the end of a relationship.

The circumstances leading up to a move will undoubtedly set the tone for the project and place a positive or negative filter on it. So, think about the root cause for this move; consider your feelings about the situation as well as the move itself.

While you may not have control over the circumstances, good or bad, you absolutely get to dictate how you approach this next phase of your life—and moving homes is truly a new chapter in your life story. New memories will be created, new routines will develop, and new friendships may surprise you. All these are true whether you're moving to another unit within the same apartment complex or relocating halfway across the world.

Gains and Losses

One thing that's indisputable: A move results in both gains and losses. You might find these regarding location, relationships, and amenities. Locational trade-offs can be on a small or large scale. Small-scale neighborhood trade-offs often translate into distance from amenities. A few examples: You move to a new house, but now you're farther from your gym and bank and you have to shop at a different grocery store. The stores are all within walking distance but they're more expensive than your old favorites. Or perhaps you're closer to the park now, but have to walk farther to get to work.

Depending on how far you move, you may experience some large-scale locational gains and losses, too. These could pertain to scenery, weather, access to activities, a change in pace from urban to rural, or vice versa. Whether you view these factors as positive or negative will likely depend on your temperament and past experience.

As someone who grew up in a small town in southeast Texas (population around 2,000), moved on to spend years in the Phoenix desert, and now lives in a rainy city in the Pacific Northwest, I have certainly experienced trade-offs. I love the people, culture, wildness, and beauty of Portland, Oregon, but I often miss Arizona's sunshine, bright blue skies, and expansive terrain. You could look into the distance for miles and feel like you were the only person on the planet. I miss the uniquely carved rock formations that appeared out of nowhere along the straight and open highways. Sometimes, I still miss the small town in Texas where I grew up: the Cajun food, the horses we rode, the hot days on the lake. I miss the simplicity of gathering around a bonfire with friends.

Remember that everything is a trade-off. Life is all about rejecting one thing in favor of another. It doesn't mean that either is necessarily better or worse, just different. There is so much beauty to be seen, and I feel lucky to have experienced so much of it.

Relationship gains and losses are generally a lot more complex and can be exciting and painful at the same time. I made the choice years ago to leave the area where every single friend and family member resided—and I did it alone with two preschoolers. This was a *huge* trade-off: In exchange for losing the safety of family support, I gained the freedom and exhilaration of forging my own path. Like me, you may be moving farther away from family and friends while struggling with the fear and/or excitement of cutting yourself loose. This could mean a gain or loss of financial freedom as well as free time.

You may also find that you're not the only person with emotions regarding your move. Moving away from friends and family can be even more stressful for kids who may be switching schools. Also, the people you're leaving behind may bring their own emotions to the table. Allow the other people in your life to express their emotions so you can support one another throughout this process.

Preserving Your Memories

It can be bittersweet moving out of a home you've lived in for a while. Even if you're excited and upgrading, there might be a part of you that also feels sad about leaving a space that has housed so many memories.

This is a good time to take some pictures of yourself and/or your family in the different rooms. Take a photo of the exterior, too, because you never know when you might want to see the house where you used to live. Snap these with a camera or smartphone and store online for later—no need for prints.

Spend some time in your home, even after it's empty, to gain closure and say goodbye. This is a positive way to express appreciation for that time of your life, for the walls and structures that kept you safe, and the memories you had there.

For the belongings that won't be part of this next phase of your life, remember that there are ways to preserve their memory, as well. Refer back to Step 3: The Big Sort (see page 11), as well as the preserving memories section of chapter 1 (see page 14) to get ideas on how to honor the memory of your belongings without holding on to them physically.

FEELINGS CHECKLIST

Moving houses can be a chaotic time with all the transfers and changes. Not only are you in the midst of making plans for the future and sometimes difficult decisions about your belongings, you're also mentally and physically readjusting. If you've already moved, your mind is getting oriented to a new physical layout both in your home and in your new location.

Because of the details and physical activity required to move a household, this tends to be a taxing time regardless of the underlying emotions associated with the circumstances. Keeping a close timeline and schedule will help alleviate this, but the fact remains that many things will need to be taken care of prior to and during the move.

That extra mental strain and physical exhaustion will leave you feeling overwhelmed and at risk of increased stress. This may be amplified by the emotions of saying goodbye to friends or family. In some cases, this rush of emotions may leave you feeling uncertain of the decision to move at all, but it's generally best to trust decisions you thoughtfully made during calmer times.

Take the time to acknowledge some of the emotions you might be experiencing throughout this process and allow yourself to be present. Understand that these feelings are normal and expected.

- Anger
- Anxiety
- Apprehension
- Eagerness
- Emotionality
- Excitement
- Exhaustion
- Guilt

- Irritability
- Mania
- Pride
- Sadness
- Strangeness
- Stress
- Tiredness

It's common to feel off-kilter during the moving process. It takes a while for our minds to process change, and a lot of change occurs throughout a move. Even for those exciting circumstances, feeling out of sorts can easily happen when all your belongings are out of place and the structure of your home is unrecognizable due to stacks of boxes and rearranged furniture.

These feelings might even linger for a few weeks after the move while you adjust to your new environment. It takes time for your mind to accept these new surroundings as a safe haven and develop the bond of "home." Even before your move, just knowing that everything will soon be different can be jolting to many people. The uncertainty of it all can bring up a swarm of new emotions.

Of course, this doesn't last forever. As you get accustomed to your new home, it will soon enough become your new norm. The more frequently you move, the easier the process gets, but if you're someone who has lived in one spot for many years, you'll likely experience a stronger reaction to being uprooted. Be sure to write down any feelings that come up if they aren't on the list: There is no one-size-fits-all when it comes to your emotions.

WHAT'S ON YOUR MIND?

Use this space to take notes, vent your feelings, or take stock of your current situation.

_____

_____

_____

_____

_____

_____

_____

_____

_____

_____

_____

_____

_____

_____

_____

_____

_____

_____

_____

_____

_____

YOUR NEXT STEPS

To avoid feeling overwhelmed by the moving process, it's important that you zoom out and try to maintain a bird's-eye view of the project. Because moving is so detail-intensive, it's helpful to break the project down into groups of tasks. Think of it as a tree diagram with different branches of projects that can be grouped together: scheduling, boxing, moving, etc.

Beneath the topic of scheduling are categories such as transferring utilities, renting equipment, and closing/opening accounts. The moving checklist (see page 122) will walk you through the preparation of these tasks, but it's just as important to keep these separated in your mind as well so that you don't get mentally fatigued. Identify beginning and ending dates on your timeline and use the moving checklist to complete the scheduling portion of your move. Follow the 5-Step Method outlined in chapter 1.

Remember that even the most exciting moves can be physically and emotionally taxing. Be sure to allow yourself plenty of rest throughout the packing and moving processes, and bring in people to help, so you can focus on the big picture. These projects typically take longer than you think they will and you'll appreciate any assistance you were able to get when all is said and done.

Whatever the cause for this move, keep in mind this is a new chapter in your story and an opportunity for a fresh start. Allow this to be a defining moment when you created an intentional home environment based on your own creative vision and careful selection of belongings.

4

Empty(-ish) Nests

THE TASK AHEAD

I read a book once about dragons that spanned miles. They were so huge that when one flew over a city, it would blot out the sun, and if it was in a particularly fierce mood, it could take out a small town in a single breath. People put them in chains lest their herds and crops get barbecued, but dragons weren't meant to be restrained. Without the ability to stretch their wings and soar, they began to shrink, until the last remaining dragons were as small as a bat and could barely light a candle with their flames.

Making room for development is an ongoing necessity for every living thing—humans, plants, and fictitious dragons. This section is for parents, or anyone filling a parental role. Embracing transitions and actively making room for growth not only allows you to soar—it will help your children stretch and mature, too.

For the purpose of this chapter, we'll be focusing primarily on empty nesters, but many of the emotions and concepts also apply to other child-related transitions. For example, you may find yourself going through similar emotions and downgrading needs when it's time to transition out of a nursery and let go of baby items, or to trade in a child-themed room for a mature teen hub. The overarching theme here is that you're making room for growth.

THE LOGISTICS OF EMPTY NESTING

Whether the destination is college, it's typical for a young adult leaving home for the first time to live in shared housing or small studio accommodations. They'll unlikely have space to store all their belongings, but they may want to hold on to them for the future when they have more room.

Since both you and your child are dealing with memories, you may need to make some kind of temporary storage agreement. This concept of shared memories from different perspectives (those of the child and the parent) makes this an especially unique situation.

The Vision

It wasn't until recently, when I came across an old picture of preadolescent *me* sitting on my childhood bed, that I realized how gaudy and unattractive my room actually was: teal blue walls and two twin beds topped with bright pink-and-white floral comforters.

My dad's a hunting man—a duck-hunting fanatic, to be specific. My entire life he spent nearly every weekend out at the hunting camp with friends. His idea of comedy was to proudly sound a duck call throughout the house. It sounded ridiculous to us and that brought him great joy.

He also loved scuba diving and got me certified the moment I turned 13. My parents' bedroom was adorned, wall to wall, with underwater diving shots—a puffer fish, full puff; a close-up of his face with giant eyes behind goggles; and a picture of him holding up the biggest lobster you've ever seen.

Recently I visited my old bedroom to discover a stuffed duck, wings spread for takeoff, on a table in the center of the room. On a freshly painted wall was the aforementioned gigantic lobster, stuffed and mounted.

My dad had a vision. It isn't any vision I would have chosen, but it's true to who he is. The room still contains a bed for me, but if he wants to sit on that bed and stare at his stuffed duck and mounted lobster all day, he's free to do just that. After all, it's not my house. In fact, I got such a kick out of this, I posted a picture of me holding the duck and standing next to the lobster to share with my friends.

If you're in the process of reclaiming your whole nest as kids move out, this is a pivotal time in your life. How you navigate this transition could set the tone for your future routines and daily home experiences. You have a unique opportunity now to create your next phase in an intentional way.

Regardless of how you feel about your child's next stage, you can be excited about creating a vision for your new daily life. This doesn't need to hinge on a single room, but one room is a good place to start. And you don't have to do it alone; create a shared vision with your significant other or bring a friend to bounce ideas around with.

Perhaps you're downsizing your home altogether and moving into a smaller space with fewer rooms. If that's the case, I recommend that you also read chapter 3 on moving houses. Expand your vision to what this new life will look like.

Communication

Communication will be a priority here. If you're downsizing just one room, a full team of friends and relatives may not be necessary. However, a team of individuals is still involved in this process—you, your grown child, and a significant other, as the case may be—so be sure to maintain open communication with them.

Don't assume you know which belongings your child doesn't want anymore, but also, don't assume you know which ones they *do* want to keep. Assuming that your child will eventually want certain things will lead you to unnecessarily hold on to stuff. But often, grown children actually have less interest in their childhood belongings than their parents do. Be prepared for that.

Once you hash out an idea for this newly vacant space, it's time to have a chat with your child about your plans. Be sensitive to any feelings they may have about losing a childhood room. Over the years, they've likely felt personal ownership of this space and developed an attachment. Look for ways to include them throughout the process if they show an interest.

Here are some questions to ask and address:

- What things do they know for sure they want to keep?

- When will they be available to sort through belongings?

- Will any storage be needed and, if so, how much?

- Are there items they would like to bring with them?

- Do they have any concerns about this change?

Their primary concern may be the idea of still having a place to come home to, so approach the conversation with solutions and ideas. Will the room be modified into a guest room incorporating some of their belongings? Could you make the room into a cozy retreat for them using a pull-out couch? Set the tone for a pleasant transition.

The Timeline

As the parent and remaining owner of the space, you might have to manage the timeline by following up frequently. It may not be easy, but try to get solid confirmation on scheduled sorting dates from your child. Be accommodating to their new schedule but have a reasonable deadline for holding their room as is.

I see it happen all too often where parents end up waiting and holding on to their kids' stuff until their home becomes a permanent storage facility for their grown children. Part of this transition includes setting new boundaries. These boundaries will likely start off soft but should become firmer over time.

Here's what your timeline should look like:

- **A pre-sorting planning phase:** Plan and develop your vision for the room (a shared vision if you have a significant other who will share this space).

- **A conversation with your child:** Discuss the belongings they want to keep and any storage agreements.

- **A start date for sorting items:** This is covered in Step 3: The Big Sort (see page 11).

- **Dates your child will help:** Confirm dates your child will go through their belongings.
- **Dates for outside involvement:** These are confirmed dates to investigate storage facilities, donation or trash pickup services, working with an eBay reseller, etc.
- **A project completion date:** This should be pretty straightforward, but be realistic with yourself about it. It takes a lot of energy to do what you're about to do, so be honest with yourself—but set a firm deadline.

THE EMOTIONS OF EMPTY NESTING

A whirlwind of conflicting emotions is bound to arise throughout this transition. One woman said she unexpectedly burst into tears on the ride home from dropping her son off at college, and within 24 hours, she and her husband caught the next flight to Vegas!

Your response to this change is a direct result of the story you tell yourself about what this new phase means. If the chatter in your mind tells you that this transition implies that you're getting old or that you're not needed anymore, your emotional response is going to be pretty grim. However, if you allow this transition to mean something else— like being free to travel on a whim, walk around naked, throw grown-up parties (whatever that means to you), binge-watch your favorite TV show, or read a book to completion in a totally clean house—your experience will be something entirely different.

One of your greatest adjustments will likely be related to your identity. Just like your profession, your parental status is a primary stream of your identity, both to yourself and to others. This will be even more prominent if you're the type of parent who has molded your life around your child's. Take the time to mentally adjust to this somewhat new identity. Decide with intention what this "new you" looks like.

Working through Emotions

Sorting through your child's belongings is a way to mentally file these parental parts of your life as well as theirs. In this way, decluttering serves as a form of therapy. As in any form of therapy, you can't work around the process, you have to work *through* it. "Working around" the process here might be throwing all your child's belongings into a box and shoving it out of sight to avoid getting emotional. "Working *through*" requires thought and engagement, acknowledging your feelings about the items, and then making choices about what to do with them.

This process might be completely easy for you, maybe even exciting. After all, the goal is to reclaim your space and create something new. There's no guilt in not feeling nostalgic or weepy when your kiddo has left the nest. Each person grows and transitions in their own way. It could also be that your transition process comes with a delayed emotional response. You might be blindsided by a flood of emotions after the fact.

All these responses are totally normal. Don't compare your process and emotions with those of a friend or family member, and don't let anyone else declare how you should be feeling. If, however, you do begin feeling flooded with emotions, take a step back and clear your mind.

Mental clarity brings hope and optimism. Some great ways to achieve mental clarity are as follows:

- **Move your body:** Go on a walk or to the gym. Blood flow to the brain and organs will invigorate you and allow a fresh perspective.

- **Talk it out:** Call your go-to friend or family member. A simple conversation with someone whose world is currently stable can help stabilize you when things are shifting.

- **Nourish yourself:** Drink a lot of water during emotional times to keep your body chemistry in balance (or to replace all the water loss from sobbing your eyes out). Eat nourishing foods known to lift your mood and energy, like berries.

- **Step outdoors:** Soak in some sunshine and nature. Nothing puts the world back into perspective like observing nature. Also, fresh oxygen and sunshine are known to revitalize and increase happiness. And if you can't step outside, at least open the shades or a window if you can.

- **Break the pattern:** Sometimes you just need to break up your thoughts for a bit. This might be a good time to go catch a movie with your significant other (or even alone) and get lost in someone else's story for a change.

Preserving Memories

Even if none of the belongings will remain in the same room, the sorting process should still be a matter of intentional *selecting*. In other words, don't box everything up for keeps just because "things are going to be stored anyway—might as well store it all." In fact, now might be a good time to pull out any previously boxed childhood items stacked away in the garage. You can go through all their stuff with fresh eyes—sorted by year—and choose only the most meaningful pieces.

Think of your plan for the items you're choosing to keep. Are there ways these pieces can be incorporated into the daily décor or integrated for daily use? What about giving them to someone in the family? Is there another family member at the right age to enjoy some of these belongings? If so, this would allow these items to remain in the family for a bit longer.

Remember that there are other options for preserving memories than keeping the item itself (see page 14). Think of creative ways to photograph things for a childhood scrapbook. As we've talked about before, photo albums, scrapbooks, and digital files are easier to access and more space-friendly than storing objects in a box. Consider this question: If you're feeling nostalgic or sitting with family one day in the future, will it be more enjoyable to pull out an album of memories, or dig out a dusty bin from the garage?

Again, the memories aren't all yours. Be sure to involve any other parent or child in the process of preserving the memories. A grandparent or another relative may also have an interest in keeping an item or two. Get creative, but remember that the belongings aren't what really matter. Don't get so stuck on the past that you forget to enjoy who you're becoming.

FEELINGS CHECKLIST

How you respond to this transition will largely depend on your personality type and your relationship with your child. There is no right or wrong way to feel. There's nothing wrong with feeling nothing at all.

Even if your child isn't leaving home, you might find yourself feeling nostalgic when letting go of their favorite baby toys and trading in their nursery for a "big kid's room." You might feel it again when they become "too mature" for their trademark superhero or princess décor. Sometimes it's the *parents* who have trouble letting go of Bun-Bun, not their kid.

When my younger daughter was born, my oldest was two years old. Until then, she had been the baby. It wasn't until I brought home my newborn that I realized how much my oldest had grown. I remember walking into her room one night and watching her sleep, observing her lengthening body and sweet face that didn't belong to a baby anymore. I'm generally not a crier, but I broke down and sobbed that night knowing those days weren't coming back and that time would pass so quickly.

You don't *need* permission, but consider this permission granted to feel however you feel—all of it (or none of it). Here are some common feelings that may come and go during this downsizing project. Acknowledge them and allow yourself to experience things as only you can. Feel free to add any of your own emotions that don't appear on this list.

- Confusion
- Emotionality
- Emptiness
- Excitement
- Fear
- Freedom
- Guilt
- Irrationality
- Nostalgia
- Relief
- Romance
- Sadness
- Selfishness
- Shock
- Strangeness
- Uncertainty

Yes, you even have permission to feel relieved. You did it—you successfully raised a human. You've kept it all together and regardless of your contribution in the home, I'm willing to bet that at some point in that time you cleaned, provided food, worried, and imparted whatever wisdom you could, in hopes that it was the right thing at the right time. Good job.

Fret not, though. It may take some time for them to admit, but your kids still need you—they never really stop. It won't be long before they call you from the side of the road and ask you to bring a can of gas because they ran out and aren't sure what to do. They'll need you when they go searching for their first home or get pregnant with their first child. In the meantime, squeeze in some time for yourself.

WHAT'S ON YOUR MIND?

Use this space to take notes, vent your feelings, or take stock of your current situation.

_____

_____

_____

_____

_____

_____

_____

_____

_____

_____

_____

_____

_____

_____

_____

_____

_____

_____

_____

_____

_____

_____

YOUR NEXT STEPS

Decide right now what you believe this change means for you. Does it signify taking better care of yourself, more travel, better career opportunities, freedom to be totally lazy, the chance to reconnect with other humans, a new romantic era for you and your significant other? You get to choose your own meaning, so let that be the theme of your new chapter.

We discussed specific considerations for your timeline in this chapter, but for more details about developing a timeline, review chapter 1 (see page 4). Grab your planning checklist and timeline tools (see pages 5 and 6) to start you on the right foot with a solid plan: Will the space be an office, guest room, fitness zone, reading and relaxing retreat?

I'm excited for you! Anyone who takes on change with intention and a plan is brave— that's you. Some people may not take advantage of intentionally choosing their next chapter. Those people may linger and let life happen to them instead of taking an active part in the process. You, on the other hand, are moving forward with a plan and resolve. So tell yourself a good story about what this change means for you and, with a few helpful tools provided here, go create something great.

5

Senior Downsizing

THE TASK AHEAD

I like to say that I've lived a lot of lives. Every decade or so brings a whole new experience, and every place I've lived has filled my life with new groups of people different from the last. If you emptied a bag of my old belongings, you'd find: the midriff shirts I only braved during my first year of college and the unicorn horn I wore every day at the Oregon Country Fair (and haven't worn since). During this time, I've been many versions of myself and I imagine I'll be many more before all is said and done.

If you, too, have been letting mementos accumulate, you may think that your downsizing mission is impossible. But I'm here to tell you that the process can be quite simple.

Here's a tip: The simpler the process, the simpler the results will be. The more you toil over your belongings and reason with yourself about why you may or may not need to hold on to something, the more you'll find yourself keeping. Make a firm decision now to keep it simple.

There are many senior downsizing situations. In some cases, it's the adult children who are responsible for most of the planning. This chapter takes into account both the person who is downsizing and any adult kids who may be involved.

THE LOGISTICS OF SENIOR DOWNSIZING

"Growing older" isn't what it used to be. I go camping in central Oregon with my in-laws who range in age from 52 to 94 and have never missed a camping trip. One of them has even hiked a portion of the Pacific Crest Trail (where she swears that she was frequently being passed by women in their 60s to 80s). Downsizing and mobilizing are all the rage, and seniors are just as intrigued as the rest of the world.

In fact, many U.S. seniors are joining the RV life after retirement. Their children are grown and they've decided to take this opportunity to downsize years of possessions and reduce the need for upkeep. Some see this as a chance to do more with their free time and take advantage of new experiences that weren't available to them when they were working full-time and raising children.

Others are trading in a multiple-bedroom home with a yard and stairs for a small condo on a golf course that is more luxurious yet requires less maintenance. This type of downsizing allows for more money in their pockets (after selling a larger home) and costs less in living expenses.

Of course, not all senior downsizes look like this. You may have chosen to move because you lost a spouse. Or perhaps your decision involves health or safety factors. You might be considering safer options like moving in with your kids or grandkids, or transitioning into an assisted living space. On the other hand, you may need professional medical aid from a nursing home. Each of these scenarios brings its own filter to the process.

Whatever your situation, make all arrangements for your new location before beginning your downsize. The size, regulations, and environment of the new location will determine how much needs to be discarded and which items should make the cut.

Create a Timeline

While this transition may be a relief and even an exciting adventure, it can also be challenging. Many have lived in the same home for decades, which can make this change exceptionally stressful, even if it's welcomed. Making such a big change later in life, along with the accumulation of years of possessions, are stressful factors as well, so allow for a spacious timeline. In short, start early. In fact, whatever length of time you expect to spend on this project—double it (if you can).

Create a preliminary space on the timeline before the actual sort date begins. Use this time for planning and cementing expectations. Also use this time to make arrangements for any home you might be selling or purchasing.

With a senior downsize, it's important to keep a structured timeline and try not to veer from it. Structure and scheduled dates are important to help break larger projects like this into bite-size pieces. Also, having a solid structure with scheduled dates ensures that family members from different households are able to contribute.

Using the blank timeline provided in chapter 1 (see page 6), mark a segment at the beginning for the preliminary planning phase, add in the start date for the sorting to commence, and declare an end date. These are the first three steps in planning this project. Once those dates are determined, the rest of the timeline can be filled with dates as they come up.

Considerations for Sorting

The first thing to consider before you sort is how many rooms you're downsizing to and from. Eliminating *any* rooms that won't be in your new place will help eliminate a lot of possessions from the start. If you're moving to a one-bedroom condo from a large family home, there's no need to store or tote additional beds, bedding, and dressers. Also, don't worry about issues like getting rid of duplicates or discarding stuff you don't use regularly—this is the part I encourage you to keep simple. Only focus on what you're selecting to keep.

Remember, *selecting* is an act of intention. There are ways to preserve your memories that don't require holding on to the original item. If you have collections or trinkets (which used to be very popular), choose your favorites and create an album or scrapbook with the rest. Some collections may sell for a decent amount of money, which would benefit you more than storing them anyway.

Make your selections based on your vision for your new space. Even if your new space will consist of a single room, that room is *yours*. What belongings will provide the most value and pleasure within the downsized amount of space? When you downsize using the "selecting" method, it becomes easier to discard the remaining items.

You may find you go through a second pass and select items to offer your family. Although you shouldn't assume that your children want all your things, it never hurts to ask. Either way, it's never a waste to give something away or to part with something you've enjoyed for years but no longer use. Those unchosen possessions served their purpose—they brought you happiness or functioned for a period of time; now they can serve a new purpose for someone else.

Throughout this process, don't be afraid to ask for help. There's no shame in enlisting physical help to move things around or technological help when it comes to listing your stuff to sell.

Logistics of Downsizing a Senior Parent

Downsizing a senior parent who has had a health decline is always a challenge. Because this change is often unwanted and can bring about some resistance, it's even more important that you give yourself plenty of time to ease them into the idea of moving into a new space. Allow them some time in the new space to get oriented and comfortable. Have them make frequent visits before the move so that it becomes familiar.

A strict schedule, routine, and timeline is even more important here. Seniors with medical conditions rely on daily structure for mental clarity and pacing. Too much change at once can cause more strain on both of you. Come into this project with patience, and be prepared to take time and space for yourself to keep from getting over-whelmed or frustrated at what will likely be a slower process.

FEELINGS CHECKLIST
(FOR AN ADULT CHILD
HELPING A SENIOR)

It isn't fun watching your parents age. Making the transition from your dependency on them to the other way around can be difficult. When a parent reaches the point of needing care, you may be placed in a position to make decisions for the sake of their safety and health. This isn't like making decisions for your own children, because this person is an adult older than you; in fact, this person used to be the one making decisions for you.

Your relationship with your parent throughout your childhood and over the years will likely weigh in to the tone of this process, as well. If you've had a close relationship with a caring parent who was always there to support you, you could experience feelings of loss and worry when helping them downsize for more assistance. If your relationship was strained, a layer of tension or resentment may also be present in the process. The mix of emotions may include:

- Fatigue
- Feeling overwhelmed
- Frustration
- Gratefulness
- Guilt

- Hopefulness
- Nervousness
- Relief
- Sadness
- Worry

Take the time to allow yourself to feel whatever emotions you may be experiencing. Two powerful and common emotions associated with this are guilt and relief. Feelings of guilt can be overwhelming, especially if your parent has expressed any kind of resentment about having to leave their home.

You may question your decision repeatedly and feel alone in making these choices. On the other hand, it may be relieving to know that your mom or dad is in a safer space and not on their own if something should happen. It might also be a relief to eliminate the need to tend to their home in addition to your own. Feel through this process and take time to process how you're experiencing this transition.

WHAT'S ON YOUR MIND?

Use this space to take notes, vent your feelings, or take stock of your
current situation.

_____

_____

_____

_____

_____

_____

_____

_____

_____

_____

_____

_____

_____

_____

_____

_____

_____

_____

_____

_____

THE EMOTIONS OF SENIOR DOWNSIZING

As a senior looking to downsize your home, the emotions you experience during this transition are dependent on three factors:

1. The situation leading you to downsize

2. The result of this situation

3. Your expectations for your future

If you're downsizing by choice, and you're selling your home and buying an RV to travel the country, then your outlook on this whole situation is most likely: "This is great; where can I buy a margarita machine?" This project is probably going to be a breeze for you, and you'll let go of things much easier and more freely.

If your situation is that you can no longer afford the taxes on your home, but you are moving into your daughter's decked-out guest room, your feelings may likely be: "Not too shabby—and I can't wait to play with the grandkids," and you'll probably be able to get on board to move the process along smoothly.

However, if the situation is that your health is declining, and you've made the decision to move to an assisted living facility, and your outlook is that "Everyone there will be a bore, and I'll never have a moment of peace again," the chances are high that you're going to show a lot of resistance to the downsizing process ahead.

In most cases, we can't change the situation at hand. Sometimes we can change the result by bringing new solutions to the table; we can always make tweaks to our outlook. Maybe that new community is also housing your soon-to-be new best friend, a hot date, a really good bridge group, or new poker buddies.

Of course, the feelings associated with these changes can go much deeper than fretting about your social life. Many seniors worry about being a burden to their adult children when faced with the possibility of moving into a guest room, or the need for extra assistance due to illness. In general, the need for help can often elicit emotions—injury to pride, a decline in self-image, or loss of independence, to name a few. Even these emotions fall on a spectrum, depending on the personality and the severity of the situation.

Aside from situational emotions, there are also the feelings that arise when going through years' worth of belongings. These possessions have become as much a part of your daily environment as the walls of your home. They likely have many memories linked to them, so it's understandable if you feel resistance in releasing them.

The sheer quantity of belongings to go through might be overwhelming and cause you to feel stress or fatigue. Take as many breaks as you need during this process, and allow yourself the necessary time and space. For high-density areas, such as a storage shed or garage, get a simple system going to easily identify contents of stored boxes. Push the boxes against one wall and start pulling them out one by one to slap on stickers for dispersing as indicated in Step 3: The Big Sort (see page 11). Hopefully, the boxes are already fairly categorized and not a random mix.

Gains and Losses

There are always gains and losses—trade-offs you must make—whenever you shed possessions or move to a new environment. When downsizing for ease and convenience, the obvious downside is that you can't keep all your stuff. When downsizing for health and safety reasons, it may feel like you're only losing, when in fact, you're gaining peace of mind and the increased likelihood of keeping yourself in one piece. Though losing some independence, you're gaining companionship and support.

Just as in moving houses, you may have emotional ties to the home you've been living in for years. Your brain has mapped memories around the layout of those walls. There are almost always ties to belongings, especially those linked to milestone moments: items your children owned or made, or a dresser passed down from your parents.

Even the most positive downsizing situations will come with some difficult decisions regarding belongings. Downsizing to a fresh new condo might mean letting go of heirlooms and childhood memorabilia. Whatever the situation, try to find ways to make peace with this reality. Are there family members who could take in valuable heirlooms? Your adult children may want some of the memorabilia from their childhood.

Of course, there are ways to digitize and scrapbook belongings and memories, as well, without keeping all your physical possessions. In the meantime, when things start to feel fuzzy and complicated, try to focus on the gains.

Emotions of Downsizing a Senior Parent

When it comes to helping a senior parent downsize, you—the adult child—are placed in the position of tending to their emotions along with your own. Managing two different perspectives at the same time—your own feelings about the situation as well as those of the parent you're assisting—can quickly become exhausting.

This may require difficult conversations you hadn't foreseen—or never prepared for—if your senior parent has suddenly become ill or injured. The weight of responsibility and uncertainty can lead to feeling overwhelmed and a sense of guilt. People in this situation often find themselves taking on the worries of both parent and child; they are anxious about their parent's safety, and simultaneously, concerned that they, themselves, are making the best decisions for the situation at hand. It's important to understand that all of this is taking place, so that you allow yourself some grace. Hopefully, you have already had conversations with your parents about this, or your parents have a living will or advance directive to help with tough situations like these.

When it comes to having conversations with your senior parent about this downsize, just remember to keep the conversation light and optimistic. There are good reasons for making this change—that's why you're doing it. If you approach the conversation riddled with guilt, the experience becomes negative for everyone. Acknowledge the emotions you're going through, and have faith that, given the current circumstances, you're doing the best you can.

FEELINGS CHECKLIST
(FOR A DOWNSIZING SENIOR)

Being human means you're wonderfully equipped with a wide array of emotions—so feel them. It's all right to acknowledge whatever feelings come to the surface. Even in the best circumstances, the emotions that bubble up may surprise you.

Let's say that you've just retired and are finally free to go forth and experience the world. This is something you've planned and dreamed about for years, and at last it's here. Even so, you may feel sadness, nostalgia, and even resistance about letting go of your old space and belongings. Conflicting emotions are common, which makes sense when you consider that every transition has gains and losses.

You may find that you don't respond to change the same way you used to—you don't react as you would when you were 20 (I wouldn't either), but that's probably a good thing! You've never been a crier, but now you can't seem to stop weeping. There's nothing wrong with you; our body chemistry and brains are changing constantly. Allow yourself to go through the emotions you're feeling now, at this age, in this body, in these circumstances. They may include the following:

- Anger
- Dependence
- Eagerness
- Excitement
- Frustration

- Loss
- Neglect
- Relief
- Support
- Worry

Sometimes we don't like the emotions we naturally feel. Maybe the situation you're facing has you feeling dependent or frustrated, and you hate feeling that way. Judging yourself because of what you're feeling—getting frustrated that you have feelings of frustration—only places you in a negative cycle. In this case, take a deep breath and allow the feelings to exist. Ask yourself why you feel this way and what meaning you may be attaching to the situation.

You may be feeling this now, but that doesn't mean you can't make deliberate choices that sway you. Only you get to decide what this situation means to you. When you apply to it a new significance, your emotions will follow.

WHAT'S ON YOUR MIND?

Use this space to take notes, vent your feelings, or take stock of your current situation.

_____

_____

_____

_____

_____

_____

_____

_____

_____

_____

_____

_____

_____

_____

_____

_____

_____

_____

_____

_____

_____

YOUR NEXT STEPS

You're ready for this next chapter, whatever it may unfold. Now it's time to move forward. Grab your planning checklist and timeline from chapter 1 (see pages 5 and 6, respectively), and begin creating the structure for this project: Assign the preliminary phase, the sort date, and the completion date. The planning checklist will walk you through some key components to move things along.

Don't begin sorting and selecting items to keep until you've solidified exactly where you'll be moving. Even if you know you'll be moving into a one-bedroom condo, the layout, climate, and activities in the area will play a role in deciding which belongings to bring with you.

Think about the amount of non-downsizing time you'll need for the project, and make sure to allow for a very spacious timeline. For example, one non-downsizing task might be to create a scrapbook or album of the belongings you won't be able to bring with you. This could take a lot of time to create but will make it easier to let items go when it comes time to sort and donate. Another task might be to digitize any files and documents to save space in the new home. Perhaps some items will be stored as part of your will or estate: Making these arrangements and documenting this process will also require its own chunk of time.

Your years after retirement should be some of the best years of your life. This is *your* time to reap the rewards of all the seeds planted up to this moment. Whether things have gone wonderfully according to plan, I hope you'll use this downsizing as an opportunity to evaluate what's important and double down on that.

Every so often we all need a fresh perspective, and nothing sheds old skin quicker than downsizing belongings that have been collecting dust for years. A full-home downsize encourages you to reevaluate past experiences, remember goals you once had, and reinvigorate your life. Who knows what you'll look like on the other end?

6

Family, Wills & Estates

THE TASK AHEAD

Downsizing after the death of a loved one is difficult enough on its own; adding to this a legal component of wills and estates can make an emotionally complicated time downright tortuous. This chapter will shed some light on the whole process, while acknowledging what you're going through right now.

Because there's a lot of legal jargon involved, let's break down some of the main pieces. If a person makes the wise choice to type up a will—which can literally be as simple as typing a document on your computer and having a witness sign it—then it should also indicate who is responsible for carrying out the wishes it contains. That person is called an executor. If there is no will or the will doesn't identify who the executor will be, then the court decides. Usually the spouse or a child will be selected as the legal executor.

So what does this executor do? Basically, they collect all worldly possessions of the deceased in order to fulfill the wishes of the will and the law. Consequently, the executor has a lot of work cut out for them. To look at these tasks in detail, the following sections will be broken down into two parts: 1) going through belongings and assets as an executor, and 2) going through the belongings of a loved one as a beneficiary.

THE LOGISTICS OF WILLS & ESTATES

I want to point out that the executor is not the same as a beneficiary (the person receiving an inheritance), although they often *are* beneficiaries, as well. For example, you could name a friend who's good at accounting as your executor, while not actually leaving them anything in the will. (Having said that, the executor does generally get compensated, according to state laws).

The executor isn't only responsible for collecting all the money, possessions, and other assets; they're also responsible for getting the will (if there is one) to the probate court, opening an estate bank account, collecting any insurance policies belonging to the deceased, and paying off all debts using funds collected in the estate account.

If it sounds like a lot, it is. Not all the necessary details are present in a will, and some policies may have been added after its creation. So, a large portion of the executor's time is spent digging for all the information.

A Timeline for the Executor

The timeline for an executor depends on state laws; some states may require completion of certain duties by a set date. The timeline below outlines the general duties and timeline of the executor.

1. Gather all information: any wills, statements, account details, insurance policies, and other papers or documents regarding money, debt, or belongings.

2. File the will at the local probate court.

3. Notify all businesses and agencies of the death and close accounts as necessary:

   - Post office
   - Utility companies
   - Credit card companies
   - Benefits and insurances
   - Government agencies, such as the Social Security Administration and the IRS

4. Read the will and determine who inherits what.

5. Collect and inventory all assets that belonged to the deceased, and manage them until they are distributed to the rightful heirs. You may need to get appraisals, especially if going through probate court. Assets may include the following:

   - Real estate
   - Shared assets—may involve selling when left to multiple heirs

6. Check your state's laws after inventory and appraisals have been collected and determine if you need to involve the probate court or if you qualify for quick and simple proceedings without the court.

7. Open an estate bank account and collect all funds due to the estate. This is a single bank account to hold all funds and policy payouts of the deceased.

8. Use the estate account to pay off any debts and taxes accrued by the deceased. (A final income tax filing is required.)

9. Once all is said and done, disperse the remaining possessions to the new rightful owners/inheritors.

As you can see, the executor is legally responsible for many things. Because of this, family dynamics can get tricky, especially if the family members don't approve of the selected executor. If there are any disputes or claims, the case may need to undergo probate court proceedings. Some disputes might warrant an estate lawyer to help defend any claims.

One nice loophole for some of the belongings is to have a living trust. If the deceased has prepared this (often made in addition to a living will), a "successor trustee" is named to take over the trust in the event of death. That person would disperse possessions to heirs directly without court intervention. The executor will still need to take care of debts and taxes, notify the appropriate agencies, and so on, but the important possessions will not be held up by the legal process.

A Timeline for the Beneficiary

As the beneficiary, you're receiving any money or possessions that are rightfully yours, either by will or by law. The time will come to decide what to do with those belongings. Depending on your relationship to the deceased and your personal grieving process, downsizing their belongings may not happen for a while.

It's common for people who are going through such a loss to ask, "When is it time to go through these things? How long is too long?" Everybody wants to make sure they're grieving appropriately and there isn't something wrong with them. The truth is, there is no "right time." I love the way one woman put it after the loss of her husband. She said, "When there's a glimmer of hope at the idea of going through their things, that's when you know it's time."

If you feel like the time is right, then you first need to decide who (if anyone) will be going through these things with you. This is, of course, after the executor or trust successor has already dispersed items according to the will and trust. There may still be other people in the family with whom you would like to share these belongings.

Let's say a spouse left all their belongings to you, so you could decide what to do with them. Now that you're ready to go through these things, you might want to invite your adult children or other family members to look through them, as well. Take this into consideration when planning your downsizing project, so you can schedule those times with other family members.

This is a good time to take a look at Step 2: Build Your Team (see page 7). Even if you're the only person keeping any possessions, you should decide if you would rather go through this process alone or with support. Some find it a very personal process to sort through the belongings of a lost loved one and prefer to do it by themselves. Others won't even enter the same room as the belongings without some form of moral support.

Once you've set your plan and you're ready to go, it will be time to sort. As always, select the items you'll be keeping first: Place a white sticker on them and remove them from the area. Not only will you reap the rewards of a simpler downsize by removing the "keep" items first, but it will be easier for others to see what's left once your mementos have been claimed.

This type of downsizing situation may call for a higher emphasis on gifting or saving items for others. The sorting method should resemble the following:

- Save for myself

- Save for others

- Donate, sell, or toss

THE EMOTIONS OF WILLS & ESTATES

Going through the belongings of a loved one is an emotionally infused time. You may find yourself looking through many emotional lenses at once, which each person handles in their own way.

On the one hand, you are experiencing the feelings of a recent loss and all the pain and confusion that may accompany that if the person was close to you. On the other hand, you are dealing with social interactions with gathered friends and family. You may be concerned with how the loss is impacting them, as well as the possibility of strife over inheritances.

If the person lost was an integral part of your daily life, you are likely facing an emotional challenge to develop new routines of everyday living without this familiar aspect of your existence. At the same time, new responsibilities and financial strain may kick in at the worst possible moment due to unexpected funeral expenses or the loss of additional income.

If this is you, now is the time to call in your support system. Don't do this alone. In fact, if you can delegate all of it—the arrangements, the planning, sorting through bills, calling the emotionally draining relative—you should do just that. Take time to rest, process, and nourish.

Everyone Grieves Differently

Let me reiterate that everyone grieves differently. This can cause strife in relationships when one person doesn't understand the way another person grieves. For some, the idea of letting go of any lost loved one's possessions can be very painful—even sorting the items may take years. Alternatively, another person might feel pain in holding on to the items and keeping them in the home. This person might be quick to let go of as much as possible in their attempt to heal and move forward.

The method of grieving and healing has nothing to do with the closeness of the relationship. Try to be understanding of other family members who don't respond to the remaining possessions in the same way you do. At the same time, don't judge your own response according to that of someone else's. Whether you ultimately decide to donate or hold on to all the remaining possessions you received is up to you—either is fine. In the end, it's just a personal choice.

Going through Their Belongings

I once spoke at a widows' retreat where the event coordinator told me the two areas she sees widows struggle with most are dating and going through their spouse's belongings. It's an emotional process going through the possessions of a loved one after they've passed.

You're bound to feel a sense of nostalgia and sadness at seeing little reminders of who they were. At the same time, you have to make practical and healthy choices for yourself. It may be that you just don't have space to keep all their belongings and are tasked with selecting the most valuable or sentimental pieces.

Try to stay away from the tendency to "box it and store it"; instead, look for items to integrate into your home as décor or for daily use. Integration is a wonderful way to keep a loved one's memory alive in the home rather than allowing the belongings to become a storage burden.

When choosing which things to keep, consider those that truly stand out as valuable reminders of your loved one. Each person has that "thing" you identify with them: the ripped shirt they wore to bed, the Rubik's Cube they constantly played with, that favorite piece of jewelry. Not all possessions are equally valuable. In fact, you may come across belongings that have no meaning whatsoever—these are easy tosses when it's time to discard.

Remember that you don't have to keep the original item to preserve the memory. Use the list provided in chapter 1 (see page 14) for some alternative ideas. Try taking multiple pieces to make one whole memory, like the woman who patched together a teddy bear with pieces of her husband's clothes. Consider creating a quilt or mural out of cloth pieces, or a picture frame out of trinkets.

Sorting the belongings of a loved one is a means of finding closure and mentally sorting through your past together. Allow yourself to feel throughout this process. Spend some time with those belongings that really speak to you and allow yourself to feel whatever bubbles up. Now is not the time to be stoic and power through—this is an opportunity for you to find acceptance and heal after loss.

Dealing with Family Stress

As I said earlier, this downsizing situation produces layers of emotion. One of those layers reveals itself in the complicated emotions that surface between family members, especially during the process of going through wills and estates.

You might find yourself in a whirlwind of stressful family dynamics, often between relatives who haven't spoken in years. This can place you in an uncomfortable predicament, even if you're not actually party to the feud. To keep the peace and prevent anyone from being exploited, you may need to interject, but try to keep things calm, if at all possible.

If the negativity becomes directed toward you or your loved ones, it's best to disengage. The hostility can lead to an already stressful situation becoming even more so. Make sure you're doing your part to understand any grieving process the other party might be going through. If this behavior seems unusual, it's likely they're acting out of pain and frustration rather than intentionally attacking you or your family.

Communication tends to be the best alleviator of family stress, but in some situations a person may be inconsolable or not so great at taking social cues. But unless you witness any actual wrongdoing or danger, the best alternative to communicating is to simply step away.

Take plenty of time to yourself to refill and reset your energy during this time, especially when any family stress is involved. Understand that this is a difficult situation for everyone and that your keeping a clear head might be the first step toward reconciliation. Sometimes a shared loss creates a bridge.

FEELINGS CHECKLIST

Your response to the death of a family member or friend is dependent on many factors: your relationship to the deceased at the time of their death, your history with them, such as whether you shared a life and space together, to what degree their death was tragic or unexpected, and many other considerations that might add to the emotional landscape.

Of course, the grieving process isn't a steady course: Emotions fluctuate, ebb and flow, and go through stages. It's totally normal to feel one way and then flip to completely different emotions later. It's also normal to feel nothing at all for a period of time. Sometimes during severe pain, our minds disconnect for an interval of time as a means of protection—there's nothing wrong with you if you notice this taking place.

Going through the belongings you inherited may also bring emotions to the surface all over again, even if you've already gone through the grieving process. Take the time to breathe and process your feelings during these times.

Unfortunately, when it comes to money and assets, squabbling and family strife isn't uncommon. The findings of a will or estate may leave some family members feeling shocked or angered or even saddened if they have been forgotten. Skepticism also rises between family members who would otherwise support one another. This aspect of human nature can add an entirely different pool of emotions and turn grief into bitterness.

On the other hand, parents or grandparents may leave behind full homes and storage facilities of unwanted stuff, placing the responsibility of going through them onto their children or grandchildren. This can lead to feeling overburdened, overwhelmed, and frustrated.

Regardless of your place in this process, you may be feeling some of the emotions below as you go through the will, estate, and possessions of a loved one:

- Anger
- Burden
- Confusion
- Connection
- Feeling overwhelmed
- Frustration
- Gratitude

- Grief
- Hopefulness
- Nostalgia
- Numbness
- Pain
- Relief
- Sickness

If you're carrying out the tasks of the executor, you might find yourself feeling overwhelmed and maybe even confused by the process. With all of the companies and agencies you'll be dealing with, it may become tiresome and even frustrating if issues don't run smoothly. Fulfilling the tasks of an executor while in the process of grieving or trying to help a grieving family member can add weight to the duties you're attempting to fulfill. Take time for yourself during this process, and know that your diligence is beneficial and appreciated by the family of the deceased.

WHAT'S ON YOUR MIND?

Use this space to take notes, vent your feelings, or take stock of your current situation.

_____

_____

_____

_____

_____

_____

_____

_____

_____

_____

_____

_____

_____

_____

_____

_____

_____

_____

_____

YOUR NEXT STEPS

If you're the executor of the will, your next step is to locate any will or trust, if one exists. Follow the timeline from this chapter to ensure that all documents and policies are gathered, before you begin the process of accumulating the assets and debts. This will likely take a good bit of time, as many deaths are unpredictable, and the person may not have been organized or fully prepared.

If you're the trust successor, your first order of business should be to review the trust, reach out to the executor to open communication (if it's a different person), and reach out to the inheritors of the trust to discuss disbursement. You don't need permission from the executor or anyone else to begin dispersing the allocated inheritance to the new rightful owners.

On the other hand, if you're a grieving loved one, but not actually playing a part in the legal process (you're not the executor or the trust successor), your primary goal is to heal. To do that you may first need to delegate tasks to trusted friends and family. Call in reinforcements to assist with funeral arrangements and finalizing any policies.

Depending on your relationship to the deceased, you may have to weigh in on some decisions, and assist in collecting documents for the executor, so conserve your energy for these necessary tasks. While grieving and tending to your health is important, ensuring your security and finances is also essential.

The quicker—and more smoothly—a person's possessions and accounts can be settled after their death, the sooner the healing process can begin. Once a person's final wishes have been fulfilled, their memory can rest, and their loved ones can achieve closure.

7

Dividing Households

THE TASK AHEAD

Even in the most amicable of scenarios, dividing a household can be a challenging and emotionally charged undertaking. In the famous words of Neil Sedaka, "Breaking up is hard to do." Very few life experiences elicit such primal, visceral emotions: jealousy, rage, despair, guilt, or pride-swallowing regret.

So, if your world has shifted, and you've become some version of yourself that you don't recognize, well, that's totally normal. Perhaps you're experiencing a welcomed opportunity to correct course and find happiness somewhere else.

Whatever the case, our belongings tend to become conduits for whatever emotions we feel. Whether you choose to cling to them, smash them, or leave them all behind will greatly depend on the emotional pool you're swimming in at the time. This emotional status will, of course, affect the ease with which you sort and divide your belongings.

Dividing households is a unique downsizing task in both logistics and emotions. There are often legalities involved, as well as children or pets to consider. This chapter will help you navigate both the project itself and the feelings that may come with it.

THE LOGISTICS OF DIVIDING HOUSEHOLDS

For the sake of simplicity, we're going to focus on downsizing the belongings of a single household. Several factors need to be determined before you can begin actively sorting and preparing for this type of downsize. The first is to ascertain what is legally yours. This may extend the timeline of your downsizing project and will definitely impact your sorting process (in that you may have far less or more to sort than anticipated).

Once everything is squared away regarding ownership, you can consider your overall plan. Here, things get simple again: Use the planning checklist from the Tools and Checklists section at the back of the book (see page 122) to guide you through the major touchpoints. Of course, if you aren't staying in your current living space, the first question you need to answer is: Where will you be moving? Before you can plan your timeline for this project, it's important to identify some key details about your future space:

- What percentage of your belongings will likely fit in your new home?

- Are these temporary arrangements that might call for a storage facility?

- What logistics would affect your needs?

These details will influence your material needs and determine which belongings are worth keeping.

One thing I discovered is how much you change when you've left a relationship. The people in our lives make a huge impact on us, whether it's a friend, a spouse, or a child. Our moods, mind-sets, habits, and even the TV shows we watch are all influenced by those we spend time with on a regular basis.

After leaving a relationship, you may find that you develop new hobbies and pastimes. It isn't uncommon for you to change the clothes you wear, the décor you appreciate—the things you generally enjoy. All this is to say that, in the future, you may not have the same need or desire for many of the belongings you have now.

Legalities

Whether your household division (divorce, separation, or otherwise) is agreed upon and handled personally, or you're going through the legal process, you'll need to hold off on downsizing any co-owned belongings until everything is settled. Of course, you can begin sorting personal items like clothes at any time. Any specifics on where belongings should remain in the meantime depend on your state's laws, so you should take this up with your legal counsel.

Unfortunately, this period can be particularly chaotic regarding ownership, custody, and living arrangements. The entire process, including negotiations and court dates, can make it challenging to finalize a timeline for downsizing and transitioning to your next chapter. The sooner any legalities are finalized, the sooner everything can begin to truly normalize.

The Timeline

If you're coming into this having finalized all decisions regarding ownership, your timeline will depend on factors such as court ordered deadlines for moving your things, selling a house, or starting a new lease. If you're in the middle of a divorce that hasn't finalized yet, your timeline will depend on your personal case factors and may be totally unpredictable.

You and your ex may be selling your home to divide any profits and go your separate ways. In that case, your timeline may be determined by the sale of the home, which could take months. Again, all of these factors—where you'll live in the interim, what you'll take, where you'll go when it's all said and done—will contribute to the project timeline. These details will determine when and where you sort and store your things and may impact your decision to keep certain belongings at all.

Clarity comes from taking a bird's-eye view. Plan your timeline by zooming out and working your way back in. Grab your blank timeline and your overall project timeline tools from the blank worksheets in the Tools and Checklists section (see pages 6 and 135, respectively), and add the following dates to break this project down into manageable bites:

- **Start date:** This is the date that you are legally allowed to begin the downsize or the date that you choose to begin this project.

- **End date:** This is the date that the project needs to be completed (e.g., a house sale date, the start day of a lease, or a divorce finalization date). If no external factors are driving this end date, declare your own.

- **Preliminary period:** Go back to the official project start date and determine the amount of time between now and that date. Perhaps you can make use of this period before the project officially begins. Consider the following tasks:

  - Do you have any personal items you can sort during this time?

  - Will you be present to sort your personal items during this period or will you need to store some temporarily?

Those are the big pieces. Once that's determined and the timeline has a bit of clarity, begin zooming in and adding more details specific to the process:

- The "big sort" date to determine what to keep, donate, sell, or toss

- Dates for family and friends to help

- Storage or equipment rental dates

- Donation and trash drop-off and pickup dates

- Meetings for items sold

Dependents

Of course, we can't forget about the kids, if there are children involved. How you deal with your child's possessions during this time can make things either significantly easier or harder for everyone involved. The goal is to help your child feel settled and safe, hopefully by providing environments that don't require frequently lugging around their belongings.

Making that a reality will likely require having some duplicates, even if that seems silly. The number of duplicates needed depends on the split in custody. In all cases, there should be toiletries for each home: toothbrush, shampoo, soap, and so on. This way the kids don't feel like they're packing for camp every time they transition from one house to the other.

Other categories like school clothes and sports gear may depend on the custody split. If one parent is covering school days, it makes sense for the school-related belongings to stay in that location. In other words, the belongings you select to keep at your home will generally depend on your schedule with your child.

It sounds like a lot to keep track of, but once everything is settled and new routines are in place, this will become the new norm. The transitions between parents may even become something they look forward to—at least, that's been my experience.

Pets

Shared custody of a pet is less common, but it does happen. Pet sharing may not require downsizing, just preparation for easy transport. The easiest method is to assemble a pet bag carrying their favorite toys, treats, leash, etc. Depending on your pet's age and temperament, keeping some regularity with toys, leashes, and food can make this transition easier for them.

THE EMOTIONS OF DIVIDING HOUSEHOLDS

Working through the emotions of a divided household is a highly personal process. So, if you're listening to sad love songs on repeat—"*When a heart breaks, no, it don't break even*"—and binge-watching breakup movies, there's no shame in that. And if you're grabbing your morning latte and going about your business as if nothing's changed, that's good, too.

The feelings you experience will, of course, greatly depend on the situation at hand. I mentioned in chapter 5 (see page 68) that there are three factors contributing to the emotions experienced in that transition; the same is true here. Those three factors are:

1. The situation leading you to downsize

2. The result of this situation

3. Your expectations about your future

These three factors combine to create your perception of this whole experience. However, when it comes to dividing households, powerful external factors are also at play, such as the emotions of others.

Think of your perception like a house, and these three factors (the situation, the result of the situation, and how you feel about it) as the bricks that built this house. It's a *new* house so you're still getting used to it, but it's yours. Inside your perception house, you're working through things—processing thoughts in your perception oven, cleaning out bad information in your perception dishwasher. You get the picture. Well, these external factors are like the weather—raining on your house and causing the occasional flood.

Instead of one person taking the lead, two people are at the top of this pyramid, setting the tone for this project—two different people with their own individual perspectives and emotions. While you may be feeling one way, the other person may be experiencing something completely different, and that incongruence can add friction and disruption to the overall project.

The only way to ease the friction is to communicate as amicably as possible. If you're able to at least understand the other person's perspective (even if you disagree) and communicate throughout the process, some of the incongruence can be leveled out, making for a smoother transition with fewer hurricanes.

Working through the Emotions

Sorting through things *physically* helps you work through things mentally. Have you ever had a lot on your mind and found yourself cleaning or sorting things around you without even thinking about it? That isn't uncommon. Sorting through belongings can help you gain a bit of closure and bring emotions to the surface that you've been diligently shoving down.

The thing about ignoring your emotions is that they're still there. They haven't gone away just because you've chosen not to acknowledge them. We tend to infuse our belongings with our emotions: each one holds a unique significance to us and calls up a corresponding emotion. The hat you wore in the Bahamas makes you long for things to be like they used to be; your ex's video game console enrages you; your wedding gifts make you feel guilty. Whatever your experience with the object has been, you'll likely feel a corresponding emotion.

Don't force down your emotions by boxing up the corresponding items out of sight. By not taking the time to process your feelings, you end up hoarding your possessions and locking them away, hindering your capacity to move forward. Of course, this directly impacts your ability to complete your downsizing project and instead turns "downsizing" into "storing." Instead, take the time and energy to process both your emotions and your belongings.

Preserving Memories

I want to clarify that there's nothing wrong with keeping belongings from the past. If you're going through a divorce or a breakup, your time together doesn't suddenly cease to exist. It's still part of your life experience—an important part. This is true whether your feelings about this transition are incredibly painful, totally neutral, or completely freeing. Good or bad, you've gained experience that'll come in handy later on down the line.

There's a difference between mindfully selecting particular belongings to keep as memorabilia and storing every artifact from your past because you're afraid to let go. One is a healthy acceptance and the other is denial. While denial may seem like a protective measure, it actually prolongs the grieving process and, in the end, makes you feel worse.

Children's Belongings

You or your kids may enjoy looking back on some things later when the situation isn't so fresh. Be sure to include your kids (if any) in this process as well. Remember, these memories aren't all yours and there may be belongings your kids want to keep in order to preserve their own memories. While you may not want these decorating your home, you can work on a compromise, such as using a memory box or a scrapbook with pockets for items and photos.

When it comes to their own belongings, they may find it comforting to have familiar objects in their room at each home. Consider dividing their current toys between homes, if your kid is on board. This has the added benefit of making both of their new rooms less cluttered and keeps their toys in each location feeling fresh.

Throughout all this, do what feels best for you and your family. There will always be people who have opinions on how you should handle this. Well-meaning bystanders will try to project their own feelings and perceived meaning onto you, but you don't have to take on other people's values and ideals as your own. It never hurts to accept helpful advice and try on a fresh perspective that a loved one may be able to share, but at the end of the day, you'll process and experience this transition as only you can.

FEELINGS CHECKLIST

Take some time during this whole process to clear your mind. In fact, I recommend making this a daily practice, if not more often. Even if you feel fine, going through these belongings and dividing a household is an emotional process. If this is all new, then you're about to experience a pretty massive lifestyle change, as well. The combination of these two factors—enormous change and emotional crisis—can be overwhelming to both your brain and body alike.

Meditation is an excellent practice for clearing your mind. This may seem counterintuitive to processing your thoughts, but it isn't. When you take the time to clear your mind and reset, you come back with clarity and newfound energy to process your thoughts and feelings more effectively.

Another effective tool is journaling. Encouraging your thoughts to flow freely from your brain onto the page is an eye-opening experience. Seeing your thoughts written in front of you instead of swirling around, trapped inside your head can afford you the opportunity to logically problem solve and make active decisions. When these thoughts stay locked in your brain, vying for your attention, it can be difficult to prioritize and consider each one in a rational manner.

If these concepts are foreign to you and you don't consider yourself the type of person to meditate or journal, let me encourage you to rethink your position on this.

We spend the grand majority of our days in response mode—responding to thoughts and feelings as they arise. But this places all the power outside our control. It's like deciding how you're going to feel based on the weather. This makes you an emotional roller coaster.

When you take the time to consciously think about your thoughts, clear your mind with meditation, and get those thoughts out of your brain and onto the page, you're reclaiming control. Only then are you able to intentionally process those thoughts and feelings and work through them.

Nobody but you knows exactly what you're going through or how many layers of emotions you have coursing through you right now. Here are some feelings common to the situation:

- Bitterness
- Confusion
- Depression
- Freedom
- Guilt
- Hopefulness
- Irritation
- Jealousy

- Mental fog
- Nonchalance
- Numbness
- Rage
- Regret
- Relief
- Shame

You may be feeling all of these, none of these, or many more in addition. Add any other feeling that reveals itself to the list. This helps you take ownership and acknowledge what you're feeling instead of shoving it away. Nobody can tell you how to feel. Your feelings are your own, and they very much exist.

Sometimes what we're feeling brings up other emotions. For example, you may feel relieved and excited but then guilty for feeling that way; or you may feel jealous and spiteful and then ashamed of those feelings. This can quickly become a negative cycle. You can only stop the cycle by accepting the way you feel and working through those emotions without judgment.

WHAT'S ON YOUR MIND?

Use this space to take notes, vent your feelings, or take stock of your current situation.

_____

_____

_____

_____

_____

_____

_____

_____

_____

_____

_____

_____

_____

_____

_____

_____

_____

_____

_____

YOUR NEXT STEPS

You're going through a lot of changes and emotions right now—it's not easy. Because this particular type of downsizing can be an emotional tornado, remember to start with a bird's-eye view of the project to keep things progressing.

You may not feel excited about timelines and schedules right now but creating a structure to work through will help alleviate additional stress and allow you to focus on more important issues. Grab the following tools from the Tools and Checklists section at the back of this book (page 117):

- Overall project timeline

- Planning checklist

- Blank timeline

The overall project timeline (see page 135) will give you a general outline of the downsizing steps. Notice that the first step is the planning phase. This is where your planning checklist tool (see page 5) comes into play. It's simple and straightforward to check off the steps as you work your way down.

The blank timeline (see page 6) is for personal tracking—here you'll enter the details from both of the previous tools. Of course, several other tools from chapter 1 can help you complete the entire project, but these three will get you started.

Go back through chapter 1 and give some thought to your vision for your new space. This may not be the situation for change you were hoping for, but it's still an opportunity to reevaluate and intentionally plan your future space in a positive way. Remember, creating spaces that inspire you and make you happy can help your healing process—and can open the door to something new.

8

Your Next Chapter

CONGRATULATIONS!

Take a deep breath, because you did it! Whether you've completely finished your downsize and knocked it out of the park, or are still working through the steps, you have a huge advantage over most.

Most people live and operate in reactionary mode, coasting along and responding to circumstances as they occur. But not you. You've taken the time to educate yourself and play an active role in creating your own future. Take a minute to appreciate the progress you've made.

You've approached this transition with intent. Wielding your superpower of intention places you in a position of power throughout this project.

If you haven't yet begun your downsize, acknowledge the mental clarity you've achieved surrounding the project. Gaining clarity is the most difficult aspect of any downsizing situation. No matter how much physical labor or organized planning you accomplish during this transition, establishing clear next steps and expectations makes things a million times simpler. It's like dialing down a task from chaotic mode to easy.

You can return to the 5-Step Method as often as you need; it's designed to work with any type of downsizing scenario. It may be simple, but there's power in simplicity. However, some of the larger concepts—big-picture thinking like zooming out for a bird's-eye view, breaking tasks down into simplified steps, configuring your outlook (i.e., checking your mind-set), and regularly processing your emotions—are valuable life skills to use in any situation.

Life is full of transitions, and this won't be your last. Chances are, you'll eventually be reaching for this book again when it's time for another downsize. A few years from now, you may be ready for chapter 2, Decluttering & Minimalism, to parse down even further. Maybe you have young children now but at some point they'll fly the coop and you'll be turning to chapter 4, Empty(-ish) Nests. And someday, if you haven't already, you'll reach that sweet moment of retirement, and chapter 5, Senior Downsizing, will help you pave the way.

The important thing right now is that you soak up all the good vibes of accomplishment that come when you achieve what you set out to do. Take the time to celebrate that success; downsizing may not be complicated, but it's rarely easy. Following through and coming out the other side is worth treating yourself to something special.

Life can only be understood backwards but it must be lived forwards.

—Søren Kierkegaard

You don't learn from experiences; you learn from reflecting on them. Throughout my childhood, I wanted to be a singer. I would join talent competitions and perform at events in my small town, microphone in hand, swaying from foot to foot like an awkward adolescent. If they allowed kids and had a stage, I was there. So what happened to my childhood dream? Nothing.

Now, I could feel defeated and bitter today believing that I had failed and fallen short of my dreams. After all, I had a dream and I did not achieve it—but reflection paints a different picture. As it turns out, I didn't much care for practicing, researching labels, or auditions. The realities of singing classes and long hours dedicated to writing songs just didn't match my sugar-coated dream of standing in front of thousands singing my heart out. In short, I didn't really want it.

Reflecting on experiences not only gives you valuable data for going forward, but also changes the way you feel about that experience. Our feelings are fickle and can change in the blink of an eye—or a thought.

You can feel a particular way and experience a sudden realization that immediately changes that feeling. It's like when the car in front of you suddenly stops, and you immediately honk—but in the midst of your rage, you realize they stopped because a pedestrian was crossing the street. Just like that, your rage is replaced with embarrassment for honking your horn (because that honk made you the jerk in the scenario). New understanding, new emotion.

Try on some of these questions to help reflect on your downsizing project:

* Did you do what you set out to do?

* Did you manage to effectively downsize, or did you end up talking yourself into keeping and storing more belongings than you intended?

* How did going through those belongings make you feel?

- How did letting go of those things make you feel?

- Did you stick to the timeline?

- Did the project take longer than you expected? If so, what were the hold-ups?

Having completed the process comes with its own emotions. Just like the downsizing situation itself, the emotions you feel on the other side of this transition will depend on your current situation and outlook. For example, consider downsizing due to a divorce. A whole storm of emotions can surface during the process of dividing and going through belongings that were once a part of your shared home—these might include anger and sadness or nostalgia.

After the transition is complete and you've effectively downsized to a furnished studio apartment, you may experience a whole new flood of emotions, such as embarrassment from no longer living in a big house, excitement at your new single-and-ready-to-mingle status, or anxiety from the newfound silence. As long as you're a living, breathing human, there will always be emotions to process. Give yourself time to process and reflect on these new emotions, as well.

WHAT DID YOU LEARN?

I have not failed. I've just found 10,000 ways that won't work.

—Thomas Edison

Now that you've taken the time to reflect on your downsizing project, what have you learned? Think of valuable components that you can rinse and repeat or cut from future projects altogether. The whole point of reflecting on experiences is to learn and grow so that you can reap the benefits in the future. Sometimes that benefit is acceptance or a new outlook; other times it's key pieces of information that can make you work faster, smarter, or more efficiently.

Start with some of these prompts:

- What systems or methods worked the best?

- What, in the end, didn't work?

- Who helped you and what businesses or organizations did you involve? (Rentals, donations, etc.)

- Would you use the same businesses in the future?

- What items were the most difficult to get rid of?

- What type of items did you notice you have in excess?

- What would have made the process faster?

- Who was the most helpful?

- What supplies worked really well?

- How much time did you end up needing to complete the process?

- What problems occurred and how did you fix them?

Imagine what we could accomplish if we approached all of life's experiences with the attitude and curiosity of Thomas Edison. Take the light bulb, for instance. While Edison didn't invent it, as is so often thought—the concept of electric lighting had been around for many years—electric lighting was impractical, expensive, and failure-prone. Edison saw an opportunity to make an affordable, reliable electric lamp, one that was cheaper than candles—and of course, we all know that dream failed scores of times before coming to fruition as the first commercially viable incandescent light bulb. Had he not reflected on the previous attempts by others, and learned key pieces of information (i.e., what *didn't* work) from his own failures, he would have repeated those same mistakes.

Maybe you found that the timeline you created for yourself didn't set realistic expectations. This is probably the most common lesson learned, because we tend to be overly optimistic about how long it'll take us to accomplish tasks. Your lesson could also be a positive experience such as finding a moving company that was so pleasant to work with, you can't wait to move again! Whatever the case, you will find that each downsize will improve because you are learning from experience.

With learning comes confidence. The first time I ever moved, I didn't have a clue what I was doing. Random belongings were shoved in arbitrary places and a giant cargo bag sat lopsided on top of my car. I'm pretty sure duct tape was involved. I felt out of my element, apprehensive, like a pretender: *Who do I think I am, pulling into gas stations with all my worldly possessions, checking the cargo straps, as if I had a clue what I was doing?*

Five years later I had moved about a dozen times and was an expert at playing packing-and-loading Tetris. You could see me driving my U-Haul, exuding pure confidence, head held high—*Get out of my way!*

EMBRACING CHANGE

There can be no life without change, and to be afraid of what is different or unfamiliar is to be afraid of life.

—Theodore Roosevelt

The best thing you can do for your happiness is to embrace change. Change is going to happen, but the way you respond to change is a choice. As Darwin said, "It is not the strongest of the species that survives, nor the most intelligent; it is the one most adaptable to change." So practice having a healthy level of flexibility.

You've gone through some kind of transition: a more streamlined lifestyle, a death, a divorce, a child leaving for college. Maybe you've just retired and transitioned to traveling the country in your RV. Essentially, all downsizes, big or small, result in a transformation.

Oddly enough, positive change can be just as difficult to adjust to as negative change. In either case, our minds have to develop new neural pathways to compensate for new information. Downsizing certainly requires change—even on a basic physical level.

For example, you may have moved from a ground-level residence to a place with stairs. Decluttering your home may also lead to new walkways, new modes of interacting with your spaces, and different daily activities. Of course, you may have days when you miss an old neighborhood or a favorite walking or driving route, but remember that, if you've moved, a new home will contain new favorite spaces and satisfying routines that you have yet to discover.

Now that you've finished this downsizing project, you may be experiencing many aspects of change in your life, all happening at once—and you may not be able to control this, any more than you can predict when or why you'll need to downsize next.

What you *can* do, however, is practice flexibility and preparedness. Use your tools, the knowledge from reflecting on previous experiences, and lessons you've learned from this book.

It's like I said at the beginning: Making the choice to let go and allow what's next—with fear, excitement, and hope—is beautiful. Every transition, good or bad, is an opportunity that downsizing helps to make possible.

Downsizing allows a fresh start. It helps to shed the old and the stagnant and brings unknown possibilities. That's the ultimate upside.

Tools and Checklists

FLOOR PLAN TOOL

Use the grid below to create a scaled floor plan of the room or rooms you're rearranging or transforming. Measure your space and furniture first to help you sketch your new floor plan realistically.

PLANNING CHECKLIST

○ Articulate the vision, inspiration, and concrete goals behind your downsizing project.

○ Set a start and end date for your work, including a date for each major task involved.

○ Determine the size of the project:_____(number of rooms or percentage to be downsized).

○ Develop your vision for the future space using the blank floor plan and your notebook/journal.

○ Brainstorm a list of helpers who could support each phase of the project.

MOVING CHECKLIST

Transferring services:

○ Cable/TV provider

○ Electric/Gas

○ Home security

○ Internet

○ Phone (possibly mobile as well)

Opening/closing accounts, enrollments, and memberships:

○ Bank

○ Gym

○ Community memberships (e.g., churches, CSAs, Hadassah, etc.)

○ Schools

Renting/hiring:

○ Cleaners

○ Equipment (dolly, packing supplies, etc.)

○ Movers

○ Moving truck

○ Storage facility

BLANK TIMELINE TOOL

Mark start and end dates for your downsizing projects as well as dates for specific tasks and events.

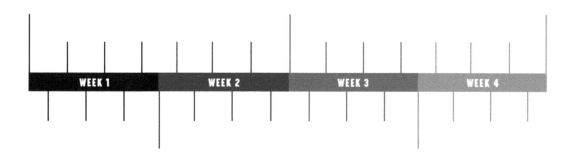

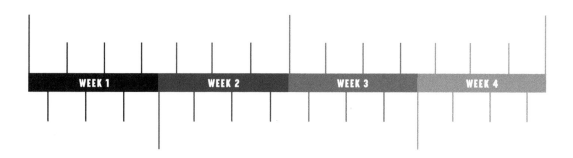

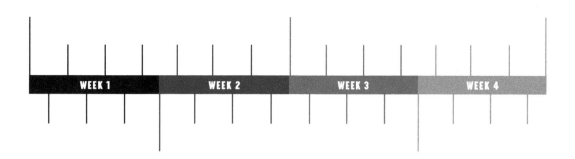

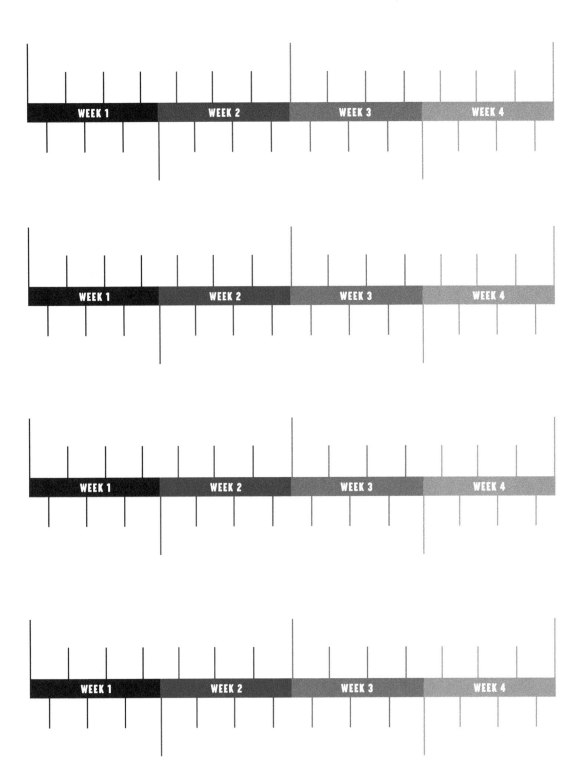

WRITING PROMPT: CLARIFY WHY YOU'RE READY TO DECLUTTER

Spend 10 minutes writing your detailed vision for the decluttering phase of the project. Think about each room of your home and how you want it to look and feel. Ask yourself:

- What kind of energy do I want each room to have?
- For what gatherings or activities will I use these spaces?
- What will be possible in my life after I create more space?

_____

_____

_____

_____

_____

_____

_____

_____

_____

_____

_____

_____

_____

_____

TEAM BUILDING STEPS

Team 1: Sorting

- _____
- _____
- _____
- _____
- _____

Team 2: Moving and Hauling

- _____
- _____
- _____
- _____
- _____

Team 3: Other_____

- _____
- _____
- _____
- _____
- _____

TEAM ASSIGNMENTS TOOL

DATE AND TIME	EVENT OR TASK	HELPER	PREPARATIONS

DATE AND TIME	EVENT OR TASK	HELPER	PREPARATIONS

TAX-DEDUCTIBLE DONATIONS TRACKER

ITEM TYPE	QUANTITY	DONATION CENTER	DATE	ESTIMATED VALUE OF EACH	TOTAL ESTIMATED VALUE

ITEM TYPE	QUANTITY	DONATION CENTER	DATE	ESTIMATED VALUE OF EACH	TOTAL ESTIMATED VALUE

BELONGINGS TRACKER

KEEPING	DONATING	SELLING

KEEPING	DONATING	SELLING

SALES LEDGER

ITEM	LIST PRICE	SOLD VIA	DATE	SELL PRICE

ITEM	LIST PRICE	SOLD VIA	DATE	SELL PRICE

OVERALL PROJECT TIMELINE: TRACK YOUR PROGRESS

- Flesh Out Your Vision
    - Define your timeline
    - Break the project into specific tasks
- Build Your Team
    - Call potential team members to get them on the schedule
    - Plan an event or meal for your helpers
    - Add the dates and tasks to your timeline and team assignments tools, provided in chapter 1
- Sort
    - Determine the items to keep according to vision
    - Place a white dot sticker on the items you'll keep and set them aside
    - Place a different colored sticker on items to donate, sell, and toss
- Disperse
    - Gather participants
    - Determine a donation center and schedule pickup/drop-off
    - Complete chosen selling method
    - Drop off tossed items at dump site
- Track
    - Track donations using the donations tracker
    - Track sales using the sales ledger

Acknowledgments

To my partner in life, Matt, who has been my rock and supported me through every entrepreneurial endeavor, including writing this book. For always being available for honest feedback, for listening to me repeatedly read sections out loud and brainstorming ideas, and for never once telling me I couldn't do it.

To my mom, who helped me co-write my first book in the fifth grade and always encouraged me to write. The woman who insisted that my fourth-grade principal allow me to read my poetry out loud because it absolutely wasn't plagiarized. If not for your total belief throughout my life that I could be a writer, I would have never tried.

Thank you.

About the Author

Mia Danielle runs a popular blog MiaDanielle.com, where she shares her knowledge of and experience with optimizing home environments, energy, mind-sets, and habits for a happy life. She lives in Portland, Oregon, with her family.

CPSIA information can be obtained
at www.ICGtesting.com
Printed in the USA
BVHW061651141219
566339BV00001B/1

9 781641 528627